A Backhanded
View of
the Law

ALSO BY MORDECAI ROSENFELD

The Lament of the Single Practitioner:
Essays on the Law   1988

A Backhanded
View of
the Law

Irreverent Essays
on Justice

Mordecai Rosenfeld

Ox Bow Press
Woodbridge, Connecticut 06525

Published by
OX BOW PRESS
P.O. Box 4045
Woodbridge, Connecticut 06525

Printed in the United States of America

Library of Congress Cataloging-in-Publication Data
Rosenfeld, Mordecai.
    A backhanded view of the law : irreverent essays on justice /
Mordecai Rosenfeld.
        p.   cm.
    ISBN 0-918024-90-0 (hardcover : acid-free paper)
    1. Law—Anecdotes.   2. Law—United States—
Anecdotes.   I. Title.
K183.R66   1991
340'.0207—dc20   91-27013
                                                                        CIP

The paper in this book meets the guidelines for permanence
and durability of the Committee on Production Guidelines
for Book Longevity of the Council on Library Resources.

The author and the publisher wish to thank the *New York Law
Journal* and *Trial Magazine* for their kind permission to reprint
these essays. The essays entitled *An Anniversary of Sorts* and *Full
Service Law Firm of the Future* first appeared in *Trial Magazine*.
All of the others first appeared in the *Journal*.

For Grandma Rose Comora
Daughter Amy Ruth, Son Michael John
and
Aunt Connie and Uncle Stu Greenfield

Contents

III. Judicial Logic, Including One Parody

IV. Judges—How They Got There and Plan to Stay

V. Reflections on Recent Wars

VI. Law Schools and Law Firms (Both Stodgy)

VII. Some Literary Analogies

ROYAL COURTS OF JUSTICE,

LONDON, WC2A 2LL

My job consists of a series of crises interspersed with complaints, in varying degrees of acerbity, from disappointed litigants and disgruntled felons.

The one bright thing to look forward to in the mail is the regular advent of the Mordecai Rosenfeld essay. I can't remember how it was that I was ever lucky enough to get on to the mailing list, but these essays have over the years been for me a source of entertainment, education and inspiration. Entertainment, because the subject matter punctures judicial pomposity, an endemic disease, certainly on this side of the Atlantic; education, because it introduces me to aspects of U.S. legal and judicial systems of which otherwise I should never be aware; inspiration, because I have to confess that I ruthlessly (and in breach no doubt of all sorts of laws) plagiarize Mordecai's ideas for speeches both lighthearted and otherwise which it is my misfortune to have to make.

That being the case, the least I can do is to give a sincere blessing to this collection of essays, each of which deserves a much wider audience than it is, I regret, likely to get. Lawyers take themselves too seriously; so do judges. If members of the profession could stand back and laugh at themselves occasionally they might be more appreciated by the public; they would certainly lead happier lives. These essays go a long way towards achieving that goal. Mordecai must be one of the few lawyers who can say—though he is far too modest to do so—that he has made life more enjoyable for his fellow men.

Geoffrey Lane
Lord Chief Justice of England

Foreword

In the bewildering day of modern jurisprudence, where all the members of any mega-law firm can hardly be expected to know each other and where the clerks are now inclined to wonder sadly if there's a life after partnership, where the computers do the law research for which the clients pay bigger and bigger fees, where an attorney general seeks to restore the constitution to the good old days of Jay Gould while radical juries take it on themselves to redistribute the wealth, it is inevitable for some of us to wonder if there is any place left for the lawyer who wishes to practice alone, with his conscience and his belief in justice as his sole guides, and who dares to assert that his profession is more than the amassing of a fortune by stimulating American businesses to gobble each other up.

Arthur Train in the 1920s created the lovable figure of Ephraim Tutt whose rolltop desk and Lincolnesque plainness of looks and speech expressed his opposition to all that was hard and slick and up-to-date in the then practice of law. Mordecai Rosenfeld is something of an Ephraim Tutt for our day. Through the years he has practiced without either a partner or an associate, determined to be in sole charge of his destiny, with the privilege of never having to compromise his own high standards of what he owes a noble profession. But fortunately for the readers of his lively columns he has a sharp eye and a biting wit to bring to his observation of those less privileged.

Rosenfeld is something of a legal scholar, but he will never allow a principle of law, no matter how enshrined in hoary precedent, to stand in the way of the rendition of what the simplest mind can see as simple justice. He is impatient with the reasoning of Justice Holmes's classic dissent in the *Lochner* case because of the great jurist's statement that, if he had had to decide the case on the merits, he would have had to study it "further and long." As it was, it was enough for Holmes that a "reasonable man" might think a law reducing the permissible hours of work in a dangerous occupation "a proper measure on the score of health." Rosenfeld deplores the cool aloofness of such a stand. Holmes, he maintains, should have simply stated: "I don't have to study this issue for one more second. It is a perversion of our constitution for the Supreme Court of the United States to invalidate a rational law that would save the lives and protect the health of thousands of vulnerable people." In the same way Rosenfeld insisted, in a case in his first volume of published essays, that it should have been sufficient, in upsetting a Texas decision sending a man to jail for life for three petty crimes (although technical felonies) involving a total sum of three hundred dollars, for the Supreme Court to have declared the penalty unconstitutional simply "because this is the United States!"

Rosenfeld can never get over the fact that our constitution in its original form, and for almost a century after its adoption, condoned slavery. One of his most charming pieces concerns George Mason, a Virginia delegate to the Constitutional Convention in Philadelphia, who refused to vote for the document for just this reason, scorning to go along with the argument of Benjamin Franklin that the proposed draft was as good as could be done under the circumstances. Our columnist delightfully fantasizes Mason running for president in 1988 and losing (despite a resemblance to Clark Gable which might have been expected to help with the women's vote) because of his anti-constitution stand. The Philadelphia compromise is to Rosenfeld a solemn warning that no document, however sacrosanct, should be allowed to prevail over a single basic human right.

Louis Auchincloss

Preface
How I Came to
Ox Bow Press

I was advised that only a university press would publish the essays in this book—the University of Georgia Press had published my first collection—and that Yale University Press was the very best there was. Being myself a graduate of its law school, and having the gracious endorsement of Guido Calabresi, Yale Law School's dean, I was emboldened to forward the pieces to New Haven. The essays, said Yale University Press, were "comic, ironic, lively, irreverent, filled with the sense of the absurd, very funny, swiping, mocking, poignant, and marked by jabs at legal idiocies;" hence they were rejected. According to the letter sent to me by an editor, the Press' Committee on Publications "would be alarmed" if Yale were even to consider publishing a book of essays so described.

But since Yale University Press was the very, very best, I decided to revise my essays so as to conform to the Press' impeccable standards. I made them dull, boring, pointless, tedious, wearisome, flat, tiresome, spiritless, long-winded and fatiguing, and then resubmitted them. Shortly thereafter I received another rejection, this time being advised that although the essays were, indeed, dull, boring, pointless, tedious, wearisome, flat, tiresome, spiritless, long-winded and fatiguing, the Committee on Publications felt that they weren't dull, boring, pointless, tedious, wearisome, flat, tiresome, spiritless, long-winded and fatiguing *enough*. I thought that I finally understood their point, so I edited them anew, this time using a thick black pencil instead of a thin blue one, slashing the sentences with a razor instead of cutting them with a scissor, throwing the unused portions down the incinerator instead of piling them neatly in the wastepaper basket, and recasting the language in a way that, I hoped, would be dull enough to comply with Yale University Press' impeccable standards. But again they were rejected, because while this time the Committee found the essays to be dull, boring, pointless, tedious, wearisome, flat, tiresome, spiritless, long-winded and fatiguing enough to comply with the Press' impeccable principles, there was no separate and distinct finding that they were also monotonous, and that, according to one editor, was fatal. Because Yale University Press is considered to be the very, very best I was saddened by its rejection. But I resolved, nonetheless, not to give up my search for a publisher.

*   *   *

When I was a boy, a big joke was "New York is the largest city in the world. What is next to the largest?" Some would answer "Chicago," and others, showing off their sophistication, would respond "London." The correct answer was then, and is now, "Yonkers," which borders New York to the north.

Yale University Press is the finest there is. When scorned by Yale I sought to be published by the next to the best; and so I sent the essays to Ox Bow Press, which is located in Woodbridge, Connecticut, the town that borders New Haven to the northwest.

MORDECAI ROSENFELD   New York City, 1992

A Backhanded
View of
the Law

I
Some Personal Experiences Recalled

A Backhanded View of the Law

Of Ivan Lendl, Louis XVI, and Lyn Nofziger, tennis has done well only by Mr. Lendl. And it is not only because among these three Lendl has the best forehand. King Louis drove the Third Estate out of Versailles and onto some all-weather Har Tru courts, whereupon they pledged their famous Tennis Court Oath, and so began the French Revolution.

And Lyn Nofziger, an official in the Reagan Administration, was convicted of violating the Ethics in Government Act for having discussed government contracts for his private clients with White House personnel too soon (within the prohibited one year) after leaving office. Those clients included Wedtech Corporation, a maritime engineers' union, and the manufacturer of the Air Force's A-10 antitank plane.

One of the high spots of the Nofziger trial concerned his continued use, after his tenure, of his White House tennis court permit. Imagine how impressed a client would be if an errant lob were to bounce through an open window, only to be tossed back by the President himself, or the First Lady, or perhaps the Australian Ambassador. "Lyn, is this your Wilson with the three dots?" "Thank you, Mr. President. And by the way, sir, Wedtech makes a very fine product line. If you have a moment, may I show you a few samples?"

3

Or perhaps, if the ball is retrieved by a braided Air Force general: "Sir, that toss is so firm, so straight, it could stop dead in its tracks any tank in the Soviet arsenal. But, sir, since you yourself may not be available when the Soviet invasion begins, wouldn't it be prudent, as a backup, if there were several more A-10 antitank planes in our fleet."

The point is that Mr. Nofziger treats the law as if it were a game. And since he is so upper middle-class, that game is tennis. If the Congress serves up a statute to govern our nation, he thinks that he alone is free to get around the law with a passing shot down the line. Or he might try a lob, going over the law's head. Or perhaps a chopper just over the net, just beyond the law's reach.

After his conviction, Mr. Nofziger described the ethics statute as "a lousy law," which it may or may not be. But if you hit a tennis ball too long, even by just a little bit, it is out and you have lost the point. There's no point arguing that the court is too short, that the dimensions are "lousy." So I do not understand that Nofziger defense but, probably, neither does anyone else. And the jury did convict.

Questionable business dealings aside, I do understand the lure of the manicured White House courts. I was once something of a tennis buff myself, but the courts I played on were rougher. I was introduced to the sport at camp (Camp Nahar on Schroon Lake) where, when the handyman was busy elsewhere, campers rolled the clay themselves. It was hard and dull work, and I became less and less finicky about a little sand here and there.

Although my backhand was weak, I was good enough to play on my high school (Midwood High, Brooklyn) team. Although Midwood had a tennis team, it did not have tennis courts. The school rented a few on off-hours at Avenue I and Nostrand Avenue; I think they were called the Sterling Courts, but I'm not sure about that and can't verify the name because there is a large apartment building there now. Those courts would be considered too creviced even were they on the moon, but we managed. It gave us a strong home-court advantage because rival teams were apoplectic about the bounces.

When I moved to Washington Heights in Manhattan, I began to play on the city's public courts along the Hudson River, just a few yards south of the George Washington Bridge. Those courts were concrete, and neither the fuzz on the tennis balls nor the soles of your feet could go for more than a set without fraying.

So I appreciate Lyn Nofziger's desire to play at the White House. The problem is not that he is no Ivan Lendl, for that category includes everybody. And it is not that his backhand is weak, a problem I know all too well. The problem is that as weak as his backhand is, being backhanded is his whole game. Or so the jury found.

May 23, 1988

My
First
Case

My first case involved a dog and a state senator from the Bronx, two barkers from the old school. It took place some thirty years ago, and I don't recall either's name, although I think the dog answered to "Robbin."

Robbin belonged to my brother and his wife when they lived in the Riverdale section of the Bronx, just a few hundred yards north of Manhattan. They regularly shopped at a Grand Union supermarket on Broadway and the 230s. There was a hitching post—maybe it was just a parking meter, if there were parking meters then—to which shoppers tied their dogs. But on rainy days the Grand Union permitted customers to tie their dogs to a pole on the inside, and so began the legal saga that is the subject of this essay. Barking and stretching his (or her) tether to the limit, Robbin apparently caused a woman shopper to fall. Whether she actually tripped over the rope or fell in a swerving attempt to avoid the hitherto-unseen rascal has never been clear from the evidence. But no matter; when she fell she fractured, or broke, one finger. A few days later my sister-in-law and the Grand Union were each served with a summons and complaint seeking, on behalf of the hapless victim, compensation of $6,000, then the limit (as I recall) of the Civil Court's jurisdiction. The possibility, however remote, of a $6,000 judgment was a family nightmare. And so they turned to me, a very recent law school graduate, to defend them. Although I was then working for a small law firm that specialized in corporate law, I undertook the assignment because I had already been designated, despite my complete inexperience, as the family lawyer. There is no task in life more thankless than being the family lawyer, unless it's being the family driver.

I studied the complaint, the first one of its kind that I had ever seen, to see how an injury to a housewife's one finger could result in the claim of damages of $6,000. The key allegation was that the injury had resulted in a lack of consortium. I had thought that consortium was the polite, legalese phrase for sexual relations, and I was baffled at the claimed connection between it and the alleged injury. But that was then, a different world, and I was too embarrassed to ask whether I was missing something, whether the married adult world was more mysterious than I had understood. But as family lawyer I had to respond to the immediate crisis—formally replying to the complaint—and I did what the experienced lawyers did: I copied an answer from the form book. That means that I admitted my sister-in-law's name (Rhoda Rosenfeld) and denied everything else. That answer was duly mailed to plaintiff's attorney, and nothing more about the matter was heard for years. It was all just about forgotten, when the court clerk telephoned to advise that the case would be tried the following Monday in the Bronx County Courthouse.

So began a weekend of feverish preparation as I prepared my sister-in-law Rhoda for the rigors of the witness stand. She was instructed to tell the truth and nothing but the truth, but not to volunteer a syllable more than was required. Specifically, she would, at every appropriate opportunity, describe the dog as gentle and meek. And then, in the midst of her casual, almost rambling testimony, we'd spring our case-winner: she would reach into her purse and, as if by chance, pull out a picture of Robbin. The picture we would plant showed the little dog posed next to her baby boy, who was about six months old at the time of the snapshot, and was, of course, adorable in his diapers. So much, I said, for plaintiff's argument that the dog was some kind of monster.

After the jury had been selected, there was a delay of a few minutes while the judge attended to other business. My adversary was a State

Senator, a veteran (he told me) of a thousand cases. When I commented that this case didn't seem worthy of his estimable presence, he replied that because of my inexperience I had probably missed the real tragedy of our litigation. I confessed that such tragedy had, indeed, eluded me. Whereupon he explained: It was the first jury he had had in years that included a majority of white housewives ("the most generous people in the Bronx," he explained). "And what kind of case do I have," he said raising his two palms upward, "a case with an injury to one finger, now healed. I wish I could pickle this jury and save it for my next case, a broken hip with plenty of malpractice." I feigned sympathy, but worried that such a jury might, indeed, award $6,000.

The trial began and the Senator and I made our opening statements. He talked and talked about all the health codes, health regulations and health statutes that banned dogs from food stores. I spoke haltingly about the inadvertence of it all. Then the Senator put on his first witness, the plaintiff herself. She was a woman in her late 50's, and was, I thought, a lovely person. She testified about her shopping routine, about the weather on that fateful day (it was raining), and about how the barking dog suddenly lurched at her and caused her to fall. In addition to her broken finger, she had bruises "all over," too numerous to catalogue and too painful to recall. Wherever she could, which was often, she described the dog as "frightening," as "ferocious," or as "mean spirited." And, she said in conclusion, "Dogs don't belong in food stores." Since I was not sure what lack of consortium meant, or what would be her response if I asked her, or whether the matter would be thought to be too delicate and therefore in bad taste (especially with the female composition of the jury), I announced that I had no cross-examination. After the introduction of some formal medical records (including several x-rays and doctors' bills), the plaintiff rested. Whereupon Rhoda Rosenfeld marched to the witness box and our take-no-prisoners defense began.

Rhoda testified, according to our carefully rehearsed script, that she went shopping on that fateful day despite an unusually heavy downpour because she was a working mother and had no other choice of time. As an aside to the jury, she added that she still worked at the very same job.

Our point was underscored when the Senator, with a politician's flourish, moved to strike her statement on her current employment as irrelevant. The objection was sustained, but I was proud that we had made our lack-of-riches point. It was, I thought, worthy of the Senator himself. Rhoda then recounted how she had tied up her little pet where other dogs were tied. When asked to describe Robbin she replied that he (or she) was very small and very gentle and very friendly. In the midst of her benign description she began to fumble in her purse with the offhand comment that maybe she might even have a picture. "Oh yes, I've found one. That's my Robbin (pointing to the dog in a bow) and that's my Joel Benjamin" (pointing to the diaper-clad infant sitting next to it). The picture was given to the jury for their further study. And defendant Rhoda Rosenfeld rested.

The Senator's summation was a rhetorical recitation of all the codes and regulations and statutes that prohibited dogs—except for seeing eye dogs—from lolling about in food stores. He reminded the jurors that if there had not been a blatant violation of the law there would have been no injury. My summation was more tentative. I suggested that since there were other animals tied to the same post, the plaintiff must have seen them. In any event, we were most sorry for the accident, were very glad that the injury had been so slight, and were relieved to learn that there had been a full recovery.

The judge's charge to the jury was almost a word-for-word repetition of the Senator's summation. The jurors were advised that if they found that the dog had been on the premises illegally then they *must* find for the plaintiff. My spirits sagged, for the trial seemed to have slipped away with the judge's brisk instructions.

Then the jury filed out to deliberate. Not much later—surely less than an hour—they returned with their verdict: $600 against the Grand Union; nothing against Rhoda Rosenfeld.

The Senator was quite agitated, and with the Court's permission, he spoke to the jurors. Had they not listened to the judge's charge about the health code violations? As the colloquy continued I became nervous—never having been at a trial before—that perhaps the jurors might change their vote. I thought that the best thing I could do, before it all unravelled, was to leave swiftly and silently. As I neared the door the forewoman of the jury called after me, and how I wished I'd left sooner.

"Mordecai," she said as I turned around, "give the little darlings a hug for me."

Hearing that, even the Senator acknowledged defeat, and we walked toward the elevator together. He then asked me a strange question, whether the picture I had produced was really of the dog in question and my nephew. It was, of course; but something prompted me to say "No." "I didn't think so," he replied, shaking my hand. "A few more ideas like that and you are going to be one fine lawyer."

April 26, 1989

Moosalamoo

Vermont Route 32 is a north-south dirt road that extends for about nine miles, linking Ripton and Goshen. So even at 5 P.M. on a nice Friday afternoon there is very little gridlock. Blueberry Hill Inn, where we spent one week of our vacation in August, is situated at about the midpoint, although it may be a mite closer to Goshen. Just back of the Inn, next to the pond, begins a clearly marked trail to Hogback Mountain; a round-trip hike takes about two hours. That peak rises to only a few hundred feet higher than the Inn—a sherpa wouldn't call it a "mountain" and neither would I—but on a clear day there are marvelous views of the Green Mountains and the more distant Adirondacks. Another walk, after you've done Hogback, is to the Goshen Dam. I'm not sure if the dam was built as a reservoir or for flood control; either way it seems to be very large for a place with so few people and such small streams. That trail (to the dam) begins about a mile and half north of the Inn, about 100 yards beyond the white house with the big black dog. And if you are really eager to walk off those incredibly delicious Inn meals (which included, during our stay, blueberry muffins, blueberry pancakes, blueberry pie, and cold blueberry soup with a small scoop of Ben and Jerry's vanilla; the partridge, to show its independence, was served with a raspberry sauce) you could walk further north on 32 to the Moosalamoo Camp Grounds (about eight miles round-trip). They kept promising to tell us what "Moosalamoo" meant, but they never did; apparently it has nothing to do with a moose. Maybe it's the Indian word for "blueberry," or for "Ben and Jerry's."

"Serene" would be too weak a word, although I suppose that the scene on Route 32 is typical of August in most rural places. The only hint of controversy is in the memories of the monuments, such as they are. Taking 32 to its southern terminal, Goshen is astride the crossroad with Route 73. Taking 73 as it drifts westward, through Sudbury and Orwell, one soon crosses Lake Champlain on a ferry (the oldest still-operating ferry in North America we're told) and arrives at Fort Ticonderoga, on the New York State side of the border. Fort Ticonderoga, with its rebuilt turrets and gun emplacements dominating the narrow southern neck of the Lake, is a reminder that the Revolutionary War was fought here. It is hard to believe, even when seeing the Fort and hearing of its glorious history, that there ever could have been contention and dissonance in so magical a setting. If one went north from the Inn on 32, Ripton is on Route 125. Following 125 through Middlebury and Chimney Point, one comes to the bridge at Crown Point. Just on the New York side is a tiny historical park that houses the remnants of the French and British forts, built in the 1750s, when those two nations were warring for control of the continent. The stone foundations are on a promontory that juts into the Lake, and one would like to think that the soldiers put down their muskets and just gazed on the peace and the beauty of where they were. Another hint of remote violence is the memorial to the boys of Goshen who died in the Civil War. A small post has been erected in front of the Goshen Town Hall, and on that post, which is almost worn smooth, are listed the names of the honored dead. I have never seen that tiny memorial, either during this brief Vermont visit or during our stay three years ago, when there was not a spray of fresh flowers resting on the top, a constant reminder of those others long ago who were cut down at the height of their beauty.

One hazy late afternoon, while lingering at the side of the Inn, the gentle serenity was broken. Looking up, I saw a small bird (it looked no bigger than a sparrow, but I could see only its silhouette) attack a much larger bird (could it be a hawk?) flying by. The smaller bird was pugnacious, and kept landing on the big bird's wing. No matter how the big bird maneuvered to free itself, the little one gave chase until he (or she) landed on the big one's wing again, or so it seemed through the haze. This sky battle went on for many minutes, and I pointed it out to someone picking blueberries. She watched for a moment too, and suggested that perhaps the small bird was protecting its nest. After what seemed like 10 minutes, perhaps even 15, the birds disengaged and flew their separate ways. Although the conflict was one that I'd never seen before, I supposed that it was a repeat of a battle scene that had taken place millions of times over the eons.

As I watched the struggle through my binoculars I began to wonder which bird was right and which was wrong. Was the small bird protecting his (or her) nest and its fledglings, or was it protecting only its territorial rights? Was the large bird a predator or just an aimless traveler, wandering about on a hazy August day? It was tempting to cheer for the small, pugnacious sparrow-like creature (was it a grosbeak?), although after a while its tenacity made it seem less and less of a hero and more and more of a nuisance. But that may have been because I was getting hungry.

But now it's September-after-Labor Day, and September-after-Labor Day isn't August, and Manhattan isn't Vermont, and the East River (even without the oil spill) isn't Lake Champlain, and our war memorials (have you visited the aircraft carrier *Intrepid*?) are of wars one can still remember, and our guns are more lively than those pickled howitzers that once protected English garrisons, and a conflict here between two birds (even if one is big and one is little) does not attract much media coverage.

And now that it's after Labor Day, and the long grind until next year's vacation has begun, I miss Route 32. That's the place to be. And if Goshen's highlife is not overactive, perhaps neither am I. I've been practicing law for a long time. I've been hemmed in by court calendars and filing schedules and unsympathetic judges ("unsympathetic judges," that's a euphemism) for a long time. Maybe "Moosalamoo" is Iroquois for "It's time to retire."

September 21, 1989

From Beirut
to Jerusalem
to Brooklyn

L ivery of seisin is not a fancy description for the current Garment Center spring line. It is, rather, the ancient common-law phrase that describes how land was transferred in feudal England: the two parties, sans lawyers, journeyed together to the property, and there the seller would personally deliver to the buyer a twig or a clod; and upon that gesture the transaction closed.

The transfer of land had, in olden times, always been accompanied by symbolism and even mystique—exchanging mere oral vows or even signed documents would not do—because owning land was the only way to own something permanent, something that never died and never wandered. The pageantry surrounding the transfer of real estate was not, of course, unique to England; it existed in every pre-computer society, and even in Biblical times. Boaz for instance, confirmed his purchase of land from Elimelech when he (Boaz) took off his shoe and gave it to a neighbor (Ruth 4:7). That particular transfer technique was controversial even then (in the time of the judges, about the 12th century B.C.) because in every other society it was the seller, not the buyer, who performed the magic rite.

Land ownership and land transfer in the terrain of the Bible has con-

14

tinued to be controversial, some 32 centuries later. Thomas L. Friedman, in his book *From Beirut to Jerusalem,* quotes one Israeli West Banker as saying that his "attachment to the land is almost erotic." The book's message is that the indigenous Palestinians feel the same way about the same territory. A man and his ancient roots may be hard to disentangle, but if the problem, in addition to being spiritual, economic and historic, is also erotic, does that not suggest that the old leaders, on both sides, may be even less able to cope than we have feared?

But I do not write this to be preachy, because when it comes to being bonded to the hectares of one's past I am as inflexible as the next man. When the Dodgers left Brooklyn in 1958, carrying their blue banner all the way to Los Angeles, I remained a loyal fan. The Dodgers, I argued, were like Lewis and Clark and, if anything, deserved even more devotion for their pioneering spirit.

But every love has a hate; if that's not a rule of psychiatry it should be. My hate, the hate of all Dodger fans, was the Giants. Any admitted Giant fan in my Brooklyn neighborhood had to explain himself ("I was born in Manhattan, near the Polo Grounds"; "My father was a friend of Billy Terry's sister"; *Ed note:* Bill Terry was the Giant's first baseman in the early 30s). And although Dodger fans were proud of the fact that they were true baseball fans who always applauded a rival's fine play (Stan Musial of the St. Louis Cardinals was always warmly greeted when he stepped up to the plate, a tribute to his excellence), no Giant was ever acknowledged in Ebbets Field except with boos. Although the Dodgers and Giants both moved to California in 1958, so that the mock bitterness of their mock rivalry no longer rends the New York metropolitan area, one strange bias still lingers.

The football New York Giants are still here, and the real purpose of this essay is to explain my relationship to them. When I was growing up in Brooklyn in the 40s, there was a Brooklyn Dodger football team in the National Football League; and, of course, the New York Giants football team was their hated rival. The football Dodgers not only bore the magic name, but they often practiced in the neighborhood, on a small field just behind the Brooklyn College Library. After school (both my elementary school, P.S. 152, and my high school, Midwood, were across the street from Brooklyn College) I frequently dawdled on my way home to watch.

Everyone's favorite player was Ace Parker, the Dodger quarterback, because he was, like all of us, small. His specialty was the jump pass, and we would always cheer as he raced right, and then, just before reaching the line of scrimmage, jumped to throw a bullet pass to one of his ends (usually Perry Schwartz). And there were Pug Manders (fierce lineman), Bruiser Kinard (fierce fullback) and Ralph Kerchival (place kicker); I hope I have their names spelled right and their positions correct. While my affection for the football team was never as passionate as for my baseball heroes, I considered myself to be a Brooklyn Dodger fan for all things.

Somewhere along the line, long, long ago, the football Dodgers disappeared. That was probably 30 years ago; not as long ago as the time of the judges in the 12th century B.C., but long ago nevertheless. Although the baseball team of my childhood and youth not only continues in California, but is celebrated in literature (*The Boys of Summer; The Jackie Robinson Story*), the football team is gone without a trace. Only one legacy, except for the memory of those practice sessions, remains: I still can't abide the enemy, the New York Giants football team. Every winter Sunday afternoon I still turn on the TV and root for the Giants to lose.

Sadly, I have no team to root *for*. I once considered being a Chicago Bears fan because Sid Luckman, the great Chicago Bears quarterback of the 40s and 50s, grew up in my old neighborhood and I watched him play handball in the off-season on Sunday mornings in the gym in the basement of our local synagogue. I remembered him wearing a Bear jersey with the number 42 on the back, but then I thought that I might have mixed that up with Jackie Robinson's 42 (which I consider to be world famous) or with John Dos Passos' *The 42nd Parallel*, which I still dip into occasionally.

To resolve the matter in my mind, I telephoned the Chicago Bear office, and confirmed 42 as Luckman's number. My memory was accu rate, but having no territorial nostalgia for Chicago, I never was able to adopt the Bears.

So all that remains, and all that has remained for as many years as I can remember, is that I root against the New York Giants football team. And I do that even though I've lived in Manhattan, not Brooklyn, for over 25 years. That attachment to the land of my childhood and youth may be neurotic or idiotic or erotic, or all three, but there it is.

From Beirut to Jerusalem is a marvelous book because it deals not with official government policies and pronouncements, and not with United Nations resolutions numerology, but with the one issue that controls: how people feel. The book's strength is that it is not really pessimistic, although on first reading it seems that way. It is not pessimistic for those who are attached to the land on the west bank of the Jordan River because it offers this glimmer of hope: it makes one think.

A snapped-off twig, a discarded shoe, can sometimes affect events forever.

February 21, 1990

Dark
Tunnels

E ven when writing about Heaven John Milton wasn't playful. But when describing Hell he was positively gloomy:

> . . . four infernal Rivers that disgorge
> Into the burning Lake their baleful streams:
> Abhorred Styx the flood of deadly hate,
> Sad Acheron of Sorrow, black and deep;
> Cocytus, nam'd of lamentation loud
> Heard on the rueful stream; fierce Phlegeton
> Whose waves of torrent fire inflame with rage.
> Far off from these a slow and silent stream,
> Lethe the River of Oblivion rolls
> Her wat'ry Labyrinth, whereof who drinks . . .
> Forgets both joy and grief . . .
>
> (*Paradise Lost*, Book II, lines 575 et seq.)

For 323 years, from 1667 until 1990, that description of Hell stood as the most lugubrious in the English language. But in 1990 it was topped—if being gloomier can be described as topping—by an opinion written by the United States Court of Appeals for the Second Circuit:

In a timeworn routine of New York City Life
Each day a multitude descends
The steep and long staircases and mechanical escalators
To wait on narrow and crowded platforms
Bounded by dark tunnels
And high power electric rails.
  (*Young v. New York City Transit Authority*)

"Steep staircases," "narrow and crowded platforms," "dark tunnels," "high power electric rails" . . . is that all that these judges see when they look at the subway? Have they forgotten—or did they never know—of the subway's magic?

The neighborhood subway station of my childhood, youth, and early adulthood was the Avenue J station on the Brighton Line. From there I went to Ebbets Field (the Prospect Park Station), to the old aquarium at the Battery (the Whitehall Street Station), to Coney Island (the Still-well Avenue Station), to the 1939 World's Fair (I no longer remember the station because I rarely travel to Queens), to my first Broadway play, *Winged Victory* (it contained my first off-color theater joke: An old general recited a list of things for which, after each, he said, "Thank you, men." The last event on his list was that his young wife was pregnant, and when he again said "Thank you, men," the audience laughed. I was with my mother and I did not know if I was supposed to understand it, so I laughed, but only weakly), to my clarinet lessons (Parkside Avenue Station; I was, and still am, tone deaf. If Benny Goodman had an op-posite, I was it. Nonetheless I took weekly lessons, always trying to per-fect my rendition of "Twinkle, Twinkle Little Star"), to my first opera (*Elixir of Love*) at the old opera house on West 39th Street (the Times Square Station; I am not an opera buff, and have seen only a few operas since), to visit my paternal grandparents on Eastern Parkway (the Bo-tanic Garden Station), to the Statue of Liberty ferry (to Whitehall Street, the same Station as to the old aquarium), to the Polo Grounds, but only when the Dodgers played (took the train to Prospect Park, changed for the shuttle to Franklin Avenue, then transferred to the Manhattan-bound A train to 145th Street, then down the steps to the D train to the 155th

Street Station and the Polo Grounds, all for the same nickel), to Macy's for my first suit (34th Street Station), to the train that took me to college (the New York, New Haven and Hartford trains left from Grand Central Station in those years), to the old bus station at 168th Street when I dated a girl from New Jersey, to the Brooklyn Museum (the Grand Army Plaza station on the IRT), to my first dinner out at a real restaurant (at Lou Siegel's, a famous kosher restaurant, in the garment district, using the 40th Street exit at The Times Square Station), to Wanamaker's to buy shirts (the 14th Street Station, also known as Union Square), to visit my great-grandmother who lived at a Hebrew old age home somewhere far along on the Third Avenue El (she thought cough drops were candy, and I always knew enough to take them, thank her and put one in my mouth; they tasted awful), to my summer job as an order clerk at the Hebrew Publishing Company, when I was saving money hoping to go to an out-of-town college (the Delancey Street Station); to my Camp Nahar mid-winter reunions at the old Claridge Hotel (this one was just off Times Square and bore no resemblance to its namesake in London), to the Goldman Band pop concerts in Prospect Park, to Brighton Beach on a hot summer Sunday, and to the old Madison Square Garden to see the Circus, the Rodeo, the Millrose Meet, the A.A.U. Meet, the Knights of Columbus Meet and the N.Y. Athletic Club Meet (using the 49th Street Station; I was and am a track-and-field buff).

Except for the clarinet lessons, all the trips were enjoyable, even the ones to my great-grandmother. And on every trip I began at, and returned unscathed to, the Avenue J Station. I really don't remember if there were beggars on the subways then. I vaguely recall that there were old men selling pencils, because I remember being nervous as they went from car to car even when the train was moving, but I'm just not sure. I would often stand in the front car and look out the front window.

It was fun seeing the signals change from red to green; and it was fun going over the Manhattan Bridge, with the skyline off to the left and the Brooklyn Navy Yard off to the right. During the war (World War II, that is) it was always exciting to see the huge warships in dock. We did not own a car, and the subway took me wherever I had to go. And I often went alone, even when I was eight or nine years old.

And now the Transit Authority has promulgated rules and regulations banning begging in the subway, as if beggars could be sidetracked by the flick of some bureaucratic switch. And sadder still, the Federal Court of Appeals has held that those regulations are constitutional.

As its premise for upholding the regulations, the Court has cited the subway's "steep staircases," "narrow crowded platforms," "dark tunnels" and "high power electric rails." But those staircases, platforms, tunnels and rails about which the Court writes so despairingly are the very same staircases, platforms, tunnels and rails that I used as a child, and I know, even if the judges don't, that those dark tunnels are not at all like the "infernal Rivers" of Hell. Quite the contrary. For if Hell's River Lethe makes one forget, the subway's dark tunnels evoke sweet memories, even of my tuneless clarinet lessons.

June 14, 1990

Rudolph Halley and J. Danforth Quayle

I f the football teams took their positions for the opening kickoff, and one team (in the light-colored jerseys) lined up with 19 players and the opposing team lined up with only one (in a dark jersey), nobody, not even home-team partisans, would think that the game should proceed. Nor would 19 baseball players or 19 basketball players or 19 soccer players against one ever be considered an official league contest. Even a street brawl, were it 19 toughs against one, would be considered undignified and un-American. Only in the law can there be a serious argument about whether 19 against one is fair, which brings me to *Baker v. Carr,* one of Justice William Brennan's most memorable decisions.

The Tennessee legislature in the 1950s was still being elected in accordance with the Apportionment Act of 1901. As a result of urban growth, one vote in Moore County was equal to 19 votes in Hamilton County, prompting several Hamiltonians to sue. The lower federal court dismissed the suit, on the ground that the fairness of elections was not the law's business. But the U.S. Supreme Court, in *Baker v. Carr,* reversed, holding that the Equal Protection Clause of the Constitution prohibited such voting inequality. And so began the much heralded era of "one man, one vote," as if giving equal weight to each voter's vote was a remarkable thing, an electoral epiphany.

The right to vote, especially if your vote counts, is heady stuff. I well remember, at age 21 (then the age of majority), registering for my first election. Registration was held at our local polling place, a small wooden building that served as the social hall for the Congregational Church that was on the corner of Ocean Avenue and Avenue I (Brooklyn), and every new registrant had to give proof of literacy. Mrs. Wacke, a neighbor who had known me all my life, was one of the inspectors, and she vouched for me, noting with some local pride that I was a junior at Brown University. But the inspector-in-chief was not impressed, and ruled that being a Brown junior was no proof of my ability to read; I had to produce my high school diploma, if such a diploma I had. When I returned home to look for that sacred text, Mom said that I should also bring the graduation program, which listed my honors. I resisted, arguing that I was entitled to the same one vote whether I had graduated first or last in the class. It was an argument I lost at home, but won abroad, for while I carried both the diploma and program with me (Mom put them in the same brown paper bag), I displayed only the diploma.

And I have voted in every election—primary and general—since. That first vote was for Rudolph Halley, who was running for the President of the New York City Council.. With my important vote, added, I suppose, to some others, he was elected. He was a balding, short, thin fellow with enormous horn-rimmed glasses; he was repeatedly referred to in the campaign disparagingly as a "reformer" and an "intellectual." Those labels proved to be accurate because, being far, far too intelligent for the job, he faltered; at least I know that he never made it to the Mayor's office, which was assumed to be his goal. But the central issue of the campaign, as I now remember it, at least in my neighborhood, revolved around his name "Rudolph," because Rudolf Hess was still very unpopular in Brooklyn. To counter the candidate's possible connection to Germany, his supporters noted that Rudolph Valentino (for instance) was not German. That riposte brought some laughter to the campaign, because the candidate and the great lover, except for their first name, shared nothing. The rejoinder that "I've seen all of Rudolph Valentino's movies and Rudolph Halley is no Rudolph Valentino" was not far from Senator Lloyd Bentsen's comment that he had known John Kennedy and that Dan Quayle was no John Kennedy.

Which only proves that while Justice Brennan was able to improve the quality of each man's vote, no judge, no matter how activist, can improve the quality of election campaigns. Or of candidates.

September 6, 1990

The Rhodes
I Never
Traveled

D
avid H. Souter was a Rhodes Scholar, and now the President of the United States has nominated him to be a Justice on the U.S. Supreme Court. I myself once submitted an application for a Rhodes, in 1951, when I was a senior in college, but I was weeded out in the first round. And so no President of the United States has ever nominated me for anything; nor has any governor, mayor or alderman.

A few days after I had submitted my application I was called into Assistant Dean Sonntag's office and given advice on how to prepare for that first make-or-break interview. He asked if I read a daily newspaper, and I replied that I subscribed to *The New York Herald Tribune*. But I did not tell him that I usually read only the sports section, especially if Red Smith had a column or if the Dodgers had won the day before. We had regularly read *The Trib* at home, and never *The Times*, because my father had always insisted that there was nobody worth reading except for Walter Lippmann. I never understood that loyalty, because try as I might I always found him to be stuffy. I seem to remember that he was credited with originating the phrase "Atlantic Alliance" to describe the natural bond between the United States and Western Europe, but I thought that those words, even allowing for their alliterative quality, were rather ordinary.

When I told Dean Sonntag that I read *The Trib*, he said that I had to switch to the *Times* at once, because the questions I would be asked would all be derived from *The Times'* pages. He cautioned that if I was really serious about preparing for the Rhodes I would have to read *The Times* every day, Sunday included, from cover to cover. In deference to the Dean I did switch, because I certainly did not want him to see me carrying *The Trib* around the campus. But I still rarely read anything but the sports pages. And since Arthur Daley, *The Times'* sports essayist, was not much of a writer (in my opinion), I finished the paper in a jiffy, especially if the Dodgers had been rained out the day before.

About a week later I was called into the Assistant Dean's office again, and was asked if I was ready for the interview. I replied that I did not suppose that I could do anything in one week that would change who I was and what I knew. He disagreed sharply with that assessment, and stated, rather officially, that since I was an International Relations major I was responsible for knowing all the world's news, at least as it was duly reported in *The Times*. I answered, although weakly, that I had, indeed, as per his suggestion, changed to *The Times* which, I noted, I read every day. To which he said, rather sharply, "We'll see." I did not know exactly what he meant, but he followed it up immediately with this question: "Mordecai, who is the President of Azerbaijan?" I was startled by his inquiry, but it was not an answer I could bluff. I confessed that I did not know, whereupon he displayed a copy of *The Times* from a day or two earlier, and sure enough, right there on page 20, or was it 23, was an article that mentioned that very leader's name. He indicated that, in his opinion, I did not have a chance, what with my casual way, but he held out the hope that if I were to study the newspaper with more diligence I still might, with luck, save the day.

And so for the next week I read with the greatest care everything *The Times* had to report, from the weather to the obituaries. I was amazed to learn how many world-famous people died every single day, people I had never heard of while they had lived. And I even compiled a separate list of all foreign persons whose pictures appeared in the first section.

Finally my frenzy of learning ended, for the day of my Rhodes Scholarship interview arrived. The questions were, of course, broad and philosophical, and I could find no occasion to recite the names of all the prominent people who had passed away that very week. Perhaps I should have inserted them, for had it been a written test I would have found a way, even if only to say that of all the tragic deaths that week none had been a signer of the Declaration of Independence (that is, if the course was in American History). Very soon the results were posted, and I had not survived the first round.

An article, in *The New York Times* of course (Sept. 17, 1990, page A-18, under the byline of Linda Greenhouse, just in case some assistant dean should question my accuracy), reports that a law professor from Duke University has stated that Judge Souter was "the most intellectually impressive nominee I've ever seen." I myself have had much experience with the academic mind, and since Judge Souter has been quite evasive before the Senate Judiciary Committee I can only assume that the professor has based his appraisal on something *dehors* the official record. My best guess is that the scholar from Duke chanced to meet the nominee in some Senate byway, and asked him the following question (to which he must have been given the correct answer, or how else would David H. Souter have been chosen for a Rhodes Scholarship): "Judge Souter, who was the President of Azerbaijan on April 23, 1951?"

September 20, 1990

Watering
the Plants

There was a budget crisis, and in response the President closed the national parks. He unplugged Crater Lake, turned off the Colorado River (so that Grand Canyon would not be gouged even deeper while the issue of the capital gains tax rate remained unresolved) and, by executive order, forbade all heliotropic flowers from tilting toward the sun. But most decisive of all, he cancelled the dew, stating that it would be fiscally irresponsible to water the plants while the Nation had no plan to reduce the budget deficit.

Judging from that response, a budget crisis must be a new experience for the President, a Skull and Bones man from Yale; but I remember a few from my childhood. Every month my father would worry about finding the $65 for the rent. But never did he, or Mom, suggest that I couldn't go into the living room to water the plants. We had a tea cart in the living room, which was never used for tea because I don't remember that we ever entertained company who weren't relatives.

That tea cart, both the top and the undershelf, was packed with potted plants. It was my job, from early childhood on, to water them. We didn't have any special kind of watering can, none of those brightly colored plastic containers with a long spout. Rather, I used the tea kettle. Some plants were supposed to be watered every day and some every other day, but I never remembered which was which and so I gave each a daily little rinse. I should underscore the word "little," since I was frequently warned that too much water was harmful, even fatal.

Although it only took a minute or two it was the most serious chore that I had, and I made the most of it. We had a large Stromberg-Carlson radio, shaped like a cathedral window that arches to a point, which was housed in a heavy, very handsome, tooled wooden chest. During my watering chore I always asked for, and was always granted, permission to turn the radio on. I would fiddle with the dial until I found music, and then, to the sound of harmony and static, would perform my task. Sometimes I lingered in the living room after my work was done, and would change the dial every few seconds; that was fun. But before I did that, I'd return the kettle to the stove top, emptying it in the sink first. Spilling water on the living room rug would be, I thought, a serious infraction.

The living room of our apartment overlooked Ocean Avenue (in Brooklyn), a wide thoroughfare with trolleys. The windows faced west and the room was quite sunny. Mom thought that too much sun was not good for the plants, and so every now and then, especially in the summer, I would close the curtains for a few hours. But I was more concerned about the plants on the tea cart's lower shelf because they got very little sun, so sometimes I turned the tea cart around—it was on wheels—so that no side would be away from the window (and the sunshine) all the time.

When we had more plants than the tea cart could accommodate Mom put the overflow on the window sills. But that made for two complications: unless places were exchanged with those on the cart now and then, the plants on the sills would receive too much sun. And, as a second problem, the presence of the plants in their round pots made it hard to open (or close) the window. Since the pots, round and green, were usually wider than the sill, they were rather precariously perched. If one was knocked down (while opening the window or lowering the shade or drawing the curtain), picking up every drop of earth and putting it back into the pot was messy, especially if I had just performed my official duty.

Mom liked to put plants on the window sills because, she said, they would be a barrier to a potential burglar. We lived on the first floor, and I myself frequently entered the apartment through the window—my bedroom window, not the living room window, of course. But that was in later years, when I went to school, if I forgot (or lost) the key.

The first floor window was about 10 feet above the ground, but there was a white decorative ledge about half way up so that climbing through the window did not require a crampon. My parents moved into that apartment in 1927, and Mom lived there until 1981, a year before her passing, and in all that time never was the apartment burglarized, although I later came to doubt that having plants on the window sills was the reason. I don't know the reason, except that maybe criminals back then, before the drug menace, observed more of the amenities. After my father died (in 1971) I did install locks on the windows so that they opened only a little way, leaving too small a space for an intruder.

Each time I visited the apartment (I moved out only when I married) I would fill the tea kettle and water the plants. Mom would always note that she had performed that ritual earlier, and cautioned that I should give them each no more than a drop because too much water was bad for their health. My watering, she said, might be symbolic and nostalgic, but was not agriculturally necessary.

The President's response to the budget crisis—not watering the national parks—would have been hooted down in my family. But I do not think that Congress' alternative, imposing a surtax on all incomes in excess of $1 million, would have been supported either. My father would have protested that such a brusque tax increase would stifle his incentive.

October 31, 1990

Steinberg's
Dairy
Restaurant

In the summers just after the War, during my last two years of high school and my first two years of college, I worked at the Hebrew Publishing Company, a company my maternal grandfather had co-founded in 1900. It was located at the corner of Delancey and Allen Streets, on New York's Lower East Side. Although my salary was $40 per week, somewhat meager even in those days, I always ate lunch out; I usually ate by myself because my co-workers brought lunch from home. I would eat in Ratner's (world-famous for its dairy inventions; salmon loaf with mushroom sauce was among my favorites), or in Yonnah Schimmel's (world-famous for its knishes), or in Schmulka Bernstein's (world-famous for its corned beef).

And now and then, if the weather were cool enough for a short walk and if I wanted a special treat, I'd stroll down Essex Street to Steinberg's Dairy Restaurant, famous only in a four- or five-block radius, and only modestly famous even there. It was even less pretentious than the other dining places, with six or seven rickety tables in a narrow space in the back; the food—fish and vegetables—was kept in open compartments in the front, where there was a lively take-out business. Although the prices were only a small notch higher than at Ratner's, Bernstein's or Schimmel's, I considered Steinberg's to be the only *real* restaurant

31

among them, probably because I ate there less often; the fare was delicious and the portions substantial. Although I never enjoyed negotiating with all those bones, I always had, for my main course, fish. I had fish, bones and all, because I never ate fish at home. I never ate fish at home because Mom always overcooked it to tastelessness. She overcooked it on purpose, she said, because not knowing what that fish might have ingested in the dirty ocean she wanted to kill all the possible germs. But Mrs. Steinberg, or whoever the chef was, did not seem to be concerned about the ocean's impurities, so that the fish at Steinberg's Dairy Restaurant, whether served hot or cold, was always delicious.

About once a month, or whenever my law practice particularly depresses me, I eat lunch at Steinberg's. It was last month, on Friday, April 26 when a routine snag got to me. I had settled a class action, and all the terms, great and small, had been agreed to, and the formal stipulation of settlement had been signed (after at least 1,000 changes). But suddenly the company's transfer agent was unable (or unwilling) to find the names and addresses of the persons who were the class members, and the proceedings stalled because, under the law, all persons who are class members must be given notice of the terms of the proposed settlement. And so at lunchtime I walked through Saint Andrews Plaza, turned north on Park Row, veered onto East Broadway and, after maneuvering through several blocks crowded with Chinese housewives buying fruits, vegetables and pastries, I arrived at Essex Street and lunched, by myself, at Steinberg's Dairy Restaurant. I ordered boiled carp (I ordered it cold because I was, as usual, running late), rice pilaf and eggplant parmigiana. It cost $6.50; the fish sans the two vegetables would have run to only $4. The tables and chairs were rickety, and I wondered, as I always wondered when I ate at Steinberg's, whether they were the same tables and chairs of 45 years ago. On each table, in addition to the bottle of ketchup, bottle of mustard, the salt, the pepper and the sugar, was a narrow-necked white glass vase holding several artificial flowers. Those faded artificial flowers, which, theoretically, never wilt, did look as if they had been decorating Steinberg's Dairy Restaurant's tables since at least my high school days. I looked at those flowers and began to wonder if, on this Friday afternoon, I might imagine some mystery unfold.

All the other male diners wore yarmulkas, and all had begun their meal with a prayer. So there was an air of religious wonderment, particularly if one closed one's eyes and thought about it, even for someone as non-observant as myself. And it was Friday afternoon. I was not consciously looking for anything Kabbalistic, although I had just finished reading *9½ Mystics, The Kabbala Today*, and one of the scholars discussed in that book did live on East Broadway. Indeed, one chapter in the book is entitled "A Mystic on East Broadway," so perhaps walking on East Broadway, as I headed toward Steinberg's, triggered a mood. And perhaps that mood became even more suggestive as I dodged the Chinese, with their Eastern philosophy, a philosophy that has some of the same deep but elusive mysteries that enshroud the Kabbala itself. Who knows? Certainly not I. I was just trying to escape from the law, that most worldly and materialistic of disciplines, during the one hour I sometimes allow myself for lunch. But as I gazed at the white-necked vase I thought that those artificial flowers might, themselves, represent the law, for artificial flowers and the law were not only both man-made, but the two had a common origin: they both existed only because of Man's fall from grace in the Garden of Eden. That Garden was famous for both its natural blossoms (Genesis 2:9; Isaiah 51:3) and its Natural Law. As long as Man dwelt in its confines there was no need for artificial anything. But Man could not master his cravings, and so could no longer stay amid Eden's purity. But although driven from the Garden, Man did not give up; rather, he devised, as best he could, alternatives for his new, bleaker surroundings. Hence man-made flowers and man-made laws, which, perhaps, represented, as one thought about them, the same thing: Man's desperate attempt to emulate Paradise itself.

Thinking hard on that lofty but very confused theme did make me forget my law office woes, and I was grateful for that. Then, fortunately, my lunch arrived and I was able to push my idle musing no further, because separating the fish from the bones engrossed my entire attention.

May 16, 1991

'I Have Thee Not
And Yet I See
Thee Still'
(Macbeth II,i)

Mr. Justice Souter may have cast the deciding fifth vote in *Barnes v. Glen Theater,* but that does not make him a swinger.

Barnes upheld an Indiana statute that banned nude dancing. The New Hampshireman's concurring opinion made three points: (i) nude dancing was protected by the First Amendment; (ii) nonetheless, Indiana could require performers to wear pasties and G-strings (iii) because the state has an interest in "preventing prostitution, sexual assault and other criminal activity." This essay suggests that Mr. Justice Souter's underlying logic—that the more you see the more you become aroused—is not necessarily, constitutionally, so.

When I was a sophomore in high school, or perhaps a junior, a few of us nervously decided, one Saturday night, to travel to Union City, N.J. to see a striptease. Getting from Brooklyn to Union City was quite a sojourn, since none of us drove. But we couldn't even begin our travels until we told our parents *something*. We debated whether we should say that we were going to the movies, which would not be a complete falsehood since we understood that a raunchy movie was also on the menu.

Or should we just say that we were going to "the city," which, in the Brooklyn language of the time, meant Manhattan (and surely not Union City). Or perhaps we ought say no more than that we were going "out," which meant only that we were leaving our block, usually to our local candy store for ice-cream cones with sprinkles. I do not remember the explanation that we gave on the occasion of our hegira to Union City, but I do recall the long subway ride to the bus terminal, then the interminable bus ride through the tunnel (whether Holland or Lincoln I don't know) to New Jersey, then the long line at the theater, and then, finally, with expectations at a fever pitch, admittance through a turnstile. As soon as we were seated, eager for the unravelling to begin, the hawkers began instead. First they sold candy, then ice cream, then playing cards with nude girls (where the hearts, diamonds, clubs or spades were supposed to be), then sunbathing magazines (featuring the beaches of Sweden), and then, at last, the proof that the show was about to begin—the binoculars. The binoculars weren't sold, but were rented. You gave the man $10 and he gave you the glasses; at the show's conclusion you returned them and received $6 back. None of us had $10, even though we had resisted the Hershey bars, the chocolate-covered pops, the playing cards, and even the magazines. But the binoculars were considered a must, so we pooled our resources and shared the lenses. Those lenses were not manufactured by Zeiss, and as poor as they were they were made even worse by the years of use and scratches. Still, I thought wistfully, if only I could have seen what those glasses have seen. Finally, after a few movie shorts—and the cinematography was bad, even for those days—the curtain went up and the show—pant, pant—began. But whether focusing on one of the preliminary dancers or on the main attraction, the binoculars spoiled it all. For while the mind could—and did—imagine every kind of lustful scene and practice, the rented close-ups were of warts and acne. I remember, too, how the lady and her three strategic tassels gyrated in ecstatic harmony, and how exciting it was. But when using the magnification, one's concentration shifted to trying to see through the moving tassel strings to the artist's body just beyond. But peer though I might, I was never able to see anything real. And then, in response to tugging, I had to pass the binocs along. My memory is that the sexiest view of all, as the performers were maneuvering from this position to that, was when I closed my eyes; eyes closed, I imagined that it was Ada on stage, Ada the best proportioned girl in the class. Now *that* was worth the price of admission.

And although I haven't seen her in almost half a century, I remember Ada still, every bare inch of her. What a bosom. What a bottom. What legs. She was, I thought, what *Song of Songs* was all about. Since I saw her only from afar (seating in Midwood High School was alphabetical, and she was an "L"), Mr. Justice Souter's ruling that Ada must now add a G-string to her ensemble is, to me, irrelevant. For that one-half inch strip of diaphanous material won't interfere with my view anymore than did any of her other garments, including her brown tweed overcoat.

July 9, 1991

Bugged By
a Precedent

None of us was an entomologist so that bugs, flies and mosquitoes were, in the Brooklyn of my childhood, words that were interchangeable. And each summer (or beginning in the late spring if it had been rainy) those bugs, flies and mosquitoes were the enemy. That is why I was so doubtful when, in elementary school, an attempt was made to give those creepy critters some dignity, some purpose. The science teacher, supported by pictures and diagrams, asserted that those very insects were responsible for transporting the pollen from stamen to pistil, or maybe it was the other way around, making the new flowers that grew and bloomed. I thought at the time that those lectures were probably part of some religious righteousness, the point of which was to demonstrate that every creature was put on Earth for the common good, proving, once again, that God was in His heaven and the world was quite all right.

Nevertheless, despite the bugs' honored place in the great scheme, our family made heroic efforts to get rid of them all. Our first defense were the window screens, which were installed with hope every May and removed with disappointment every October. That screen defense, because it reflected his style, may have been devised by the eminent French Defense Minister, André Maginot. For very soon after the final one was hammered into place there were more flies in our apartment than there were in Prospect Park. Inside defenses therefore had to be erected urgently, and flypaper was quickly installed. But Mom found that to be a disgusting way to do battle, what with all those struggling and dead flies suspended right before your eyes. The next weapon was citronella, then the insect repellent of choice. But it was, every year, too smelly for sustained use; Mom would never let anyone sit at the table unless the citronella odor had been scrubbed clean. And when all else failed, as it always did, we were authorized to roll up the newspaper (but not including the radio guide), making a swatter. If a fly alighted on the wall, Mom would ask us to swing gently because she did not want the newsprint to leave a smudge.

The point that these invaders were evil, despite school lessons, was proven every year at the Passover Seder, when the 10 plagues were recited. Plague number four was flies. If the flies were so wonderful, as the science teacher claimed, how come that the Pharaoh, when that swarm of flies was dispatched his way, did not thank the Hebrews for making the Egyptian flowers bloom?

All of which is why the U.S. Supreme Court's opinion in *Wisconsin Public Intervenor v. Mortier* is so disappointing. In *Mortier* the High Court held that the Federal Insecticide, Fungicide and Rodenticide Act (7 USC §136 et seq.) did not prevent the town of Casey, Wisconsin from enacting its own local rules preventing the spraying of insects. And so although he meticulously complied with each and every federal regulation, Mr. Mortier was, nonetheless, by the Imperial Decree of Casey, Wisconsin prevented from attacking the bugs that were infesting *his own property.*

The Supreme Court, when it allowed each hamlet to enact its own local insect regulations, failed to appreciate the consequences. The Brooklyn of my childhood would have been unlivable had the local City Council passed an ordinance outlawing the use of screens, citronella, flypaper and swatters. What would we have done each summer, other than be bitten to death? That may be an overstatement because there was one theoretical defense that may have been beyond even the City Council's authority. I am referring to the oscillating fan. Some families would use the oscillating fan because the flies, thinking it was a hurricane, would hunker down for the night. I suggest that the fan defense would have been hard for the politicians to prevent because people would argue, although contrary to the fact, that they merely wanted to cool off and had no intention of interfering with a mosquito's normal flight path. The oscillating fan defense was only theoretical for us because Mom said that the fan created a draft that gave one a stiff neck.

The point is that the Supreme Court's decision upholding the Constitutional right of every town to protect its bugs, flies and mosquitoes could have extremely far-reaching, and devastating, consequences. The Court was obviously unaware of what would happen if people were denied the right to spray and swat the annoying little fellows. For instance, according to one article by Professor Stephen Jay Gould of Harvard:.

If all its offspring lived to reproduce, a single female of *Aphis fabae* could produce 524 billion progeny in a year.
(From the essay, *Organic Wisdom, or Why Should a Fly Eat Its Mother from Inside,* which is included in his collection of essays entitled *Ever Since Darwin*).

Obviously, without a rolled-up newspaper, bugs, flies and mosquitoes would, before you could say "Quick Henry, the Flit," overrun the world.

Encouraged by the Supreme Court's precedent allowing every community to go its own botanical way, the Los Angeles City Council enacted a regulation that forbade any outfielder from any visiting team from catching any flies between the hours of 1 p.m. and midnight, local time.

September 17, 1991

II
References to Classical Greece

Zeno in
Albany

Zeno first published his famous paradox in Elea, Greece, in about 450 B.C. Validation has taken a long time but finally happened in the New York State Assembly in 1988 A.D.

Zeno proved that there could be no motion because (he argued) before you could go from Point A to Point B you would first have to go half way. And since every distance, no matter how small, can be divided in half, one could never get beyond some mid-point. For all these centuries, noting that people do travel (and sometimes great distances), it has been fashionable for the learned scholars to scoff at Zeno and his conundrum. But they have all missed Zeno's real, philosophical point: Sometimes even the smallest, unintended impediment can prevent progress; sometimes the tiniest part can defeat the largest whole. One of the clearest examples is Bill No. 6927-A, introduced in the New York State Assembly (although not yet enacted) earlier this year.

That bill, officially designated the Bias-Related Violence and Intimidation Act, would increase the penalties for existing crimes if the perpetrator's motivation was bias, "in whole or in part." Bias is defined not only as racial, but includes prejudice against the victim's religion, national origin, age (defined, I'm nervous to say, as 60 years or older), or sexual orientation (including not only homosexuality and bisexuality, but heterosexuality as well). The proposed law was introduced in the aftermath of the Howard Beach case, in which a group of white teens assaulted a group of blacks with baseball bats, killing one man.

Zeno's paradox applies because Bill No. 6927-A uses the phrase "in whole or in part"; it's the "in part" language that makes this noble bill unworkable. It is unworkable because it would apply not only to cases involving genuine bias, but to every other crime as well. For instance, every crime committed by a member of one group against a member of another would be caused, at least in some part, by bias. It would be hard for some conquistador to convince a jury that he loved all Aztecs except the very one that he chanced to lance. By the same logic, every white-black (or black-white) confrontation would be covered by the new law, even if the players were not members of the Klan or the Black Liberation Army.

Focusing on the "over 60" clause, every act of violence against such an "old" person would violate the proposed law, for what thinking thug would mug Hector, the breaker of horses, when old folks like Priam and Hecuba were available?

The sexual-preference definition (Title Y, Article 470, Sec. 470.5) presents the same problem. Since every crime victim in likely to be homosexual, bisexual or heterosexual—the proposed law is nothing if not sweeping—the aggressor's motivation, conscious or subconscious, would, almost necessarily, have at least a small element of the sexual. Considering where Freud, Jung, and Masters & Johnson have led us, I would suppose that every crime ever committed since (and including) Cain's stony assault against Abel would violate §470.5. At the very least each such case would require teams of psychiatrists, with their untranslatable polysyllabic testimony.

And so we have the paradox of a bill that, because it was drafted to go the whole way, ends up going nowhere. But does that mean that if the law is to make headway it must always move slowly, that halfway measures are the most that we can ever hope for? Or does it mean, on the contrary, that halfway laws are really no advancement at all, but are just a bogging down somewhere in the muddy, murky middle of some legal no-man's land? The answer may be—and this will dismay some of those cheery, optimistic people who still think that there is some kind of legislative answer to our woe—that it just doesn't matter, because the law can never be bold.

The law, like everything else in this world, is subject to Zeno's irrefutable paradox: All progress is an illusion. If you think otherwise answer this question: How come, after all this time, we are still only here, just a few miles west of Howard Beach, not even halfway between points A and B?

April 20, 1988

As Time
Goes By

The Age Discrimination in Employment Act of 1967 would have been passed earlier (in 1513 to be precise) had Ponce de Leon been a Congressman instead of an explorer. That Act makes it illegal to discriminate "arbitrarily" in the workplace against persons over 40 years old; it should be called The Fountain of Youth Act because it is as elusive as that famous Florida spigot. The argument of this essay is that, unlike one's religion or sex or color or national origin, age (unfortunately) does make a difference.

The Greeks understood it well. Tithonus was loved by Eos, the goddess of dawn. Hoping to make her perfect romance last forever, Eos pleaded with Zeus to make Tithonus immortal; it was a wish that the supreme god of Olympus granted. But in her haste Eos forgot to ask that her lover also be granted eternal youth. And so as Tithonus lived forever, he became older and older and older. Eos still rises every day with the first faint light, as she has done faithfully since Time began; but, alas, she now retires right after the 10 P.M. weather report because her Tithonus has become less ardent.

What the Greeks have said so brilliantly is what none of us wants to hear—that we all stay in our comfortable niches too long. That reluctance to step aside has caused grief in every age, but in our time it almost destroyed the world. For instance, Marshal Paul von Hindenburg, who was born in 1847, was reelected as President of Germany in 1932, the

Tithonus of presidents; and Marshal Henri Pétain, who was born in 1859, became the head of Vichy France in 1940.

Bringing the problem up to date, and speaking more generally (we mention no names during an election year), we observe that it is septuagenarian judges who decide whether teenagers can have access to federally funded sexual advice; it is lawyers and doctors who went to professional schools when all their classmates were white males who now decide the direction of law and medicine; and, of course, it was frail, white-haired Congressmen who passed the nature-defying law that decreed that age doesn't matter.

Frankly, I had not focused on the age-discrimination law until I chanced to read a rather routine case, *Oxman v. WLS-TV.* Although the age-discrimination law is a social advance into new territory, the case shows that the legal process is still the same laggard.

The plaintiff, a Mr. Oxman, alleged that being fired from his job at age 61 violated the discrimination law, and so he filed charges with the Equal Employment Opportunity Commission, a federal regulatory agency, as the law requires. Given permission by that agency to sue, he filed his complaint in federal court in 1984. The defendant moved to dismiss the action on a variety of grounds, which the judge refused to do in an opinion dated September 24, 1984.

The defendant then made the very same motion again, and again it was denied (in an opinion dated May 10, 1985). Being as frothy as a beer commercial, the TV station tried it for a third time, but this time its motion was granted (in an opinion dated August 13, 1986), and so the plaintiff's case was dismissed. Mr. Oxman appealed, and the higher court reversed and the action was reinstated (in an opinion dated May 9, 1988).

And so after four years of hectic litigation, Mr. Oxman is back exactly where he began, except, of course, that he is four years older. Thus, the legal system has invented its own ironic twist on age discrimination: the very process that protects workers makes them older still.

But the Greeks weren't concerned with one man's personal problem; their focus was, rather, on philosophy. To them (if I read the Tithonus parable correctly) age was not merely physical, but an attitude toward life. One could be youthful by being bold and adventurous; or be old by being stodgy and dull. As Horace wrote:

Swift death snatched away Achilles in his glory,
Tithonus withered in old age.

Over the long haul of life it is, sad to say, usually the steadfast dullards who, by sheer survival, make it to the top. Just look around and observe.

As a gratuitous political aside, what makes Gorbachev so threatening to our side is that he may be the first Russian leader since Peter the Great who has a touch of dash, a touch of the Achilles. By contrast, a recent front page of *The New York Times* (July 9, 1988) had a picture of Madame Chiang Kai-shek, still active in Taiwan's politics. Am I correct that her policies were criticized before World War II as being outdated? They were probably outdated before Mr. Gorbachev was born. But this essay is about the law, not world affairs.

Only the law and the cosmetics industry believe that age can be covered over. But that only proves to old logicians what young thugs already knew—that the law is a powder-puff.

July 14, 1988

Some Things
Stay the Same

Drakon *and Early Athenian Homicide Law* by Michael Gagarin (Yale University Press, 1981) was never a best seller, for which the legal establishment should be grateful. Because had its amazing message gotten through, the law would have been unmasked and deflated, much the way that the Wizard of Oz was unmasked and deflated when Judy Garland peeked behind the curtain. Not that the law is just smoke and hokum; or is it?

Drakon, often anglicized to Draco, was the famous Athenian lawgiver of 621 B.C. While he himself has never been a celebrity, his adjectival derivative, "Draconian," has provided the law with one of its main underpinnings. Whenever a penalty is enacted by any government—from capital punishment to a $25 parking ticket—somebody, somewhere, will argue that that particular penalty is too severe. To which the instant choral response is: "It's not Draconian." Despite their constant reference to "Draconian," few chanters ever heard of Draco. In a recent poll, most legislators thought that it was the name of a liquid detergent that unclogs drains; some said it was the name of a cupcake and snack food purveyor; and a few were sure that it was the name of a synthetic fiber. But in spite of their lack of learning in classical history, "It's not Draconian" is the law-and-order crowd's automatic high-pitched instant one-note response to *any* suggestion that *any* penalty may be even slightly excessive.

Their response is based on the belief, handed down through the cen-

49

turies, that Draco decreed the death penalty for all crimes, even minor ones. As Plutarch once put it: "One penalty was assigned for nearly all offenses, namely death. . . . Those who stole vegetables or fruit were punished in the same way as temple robbers and killers."

The authoritative Oxford Companion to Classical Literature describes it this way: "Details of his [Draco's] legislation are not now known, but the laws were notoriously harsh (hence the adjective 'Draconian') with nearly all offences (including idleness) punishable by death."

And so for as long as there has been Western law there has been the Establishment argument, no matter how harsh it may appear to be, that the enacted penalty is quite all right because "It's not Draconian," i.e., because it could be worse. Philosophically speaking, that is a potent argument because it makes legislators believe that they have always been reasonable, even when enacting capital punishment. Practically speaking, it is a potent argument because it intimidates critics by letting them know that if they complain too much there is plenty of room for making the penalty harsher still. It's an argument that makes every punishment, even capital punishment, only a relative thing. It's like the device used by the weatherman when the thermometer reading in Central Park hovers at minus 10 degrees Fahrenheit. He reports, after announcing the New York City temperature, that it is minus 40 in Bismarck, North Dakota, suggesting thereby that New York's minus 10 is comfortable. The Bismarck weatherman tells his listeners how cold it is in Point Barrow, Alaska. The Point Barrow weatherman casually mentions the temperature reading on the far side of the moon. And so it goes. It could always be colder. It could always be worse.

But now comes Michael Gagarin's blockbuster book. After reviewing all the evidence, the author concludes: "Drakon probably did not prescribe the death penalty as we understand it for any offense."

What a stunning reversal of history. It's as if he had written that Thomas E. Dewey had been elected president, or that the Denver Broncos had won Super Bowl XXIV. But what will that dramatic revelation mean to the law? Will it mean that legislatures will soften penalties, that capital punishment will be eliminated? The answer is, of course, that nothing will change. Nothing of substance will change because, strange as it sounds, whether the official penalty is severe or gentle makes no difference for capital punishment; the only thing that ever matters is who is the murderer and who is the victim. In Draco's time, as now, capital punishment was never meted out when the strong killed the weak. Draco was guided by the conventions of his day, which were reflected most clearly in Homer's epic poems. When, for instance, Telemachos strangled the maidservants, he was not punished because he was, after all, Odysseus' son (*Odyssey*, Book 22, lines 465–72). Nor was Odysseus himself punished when he killed Hector's young son, Astyanax. Since nothing has changed in 26 centuries, Draco's improved standing with a few liberal academicians can surely have little effect.

But, of course, since Mr. Gagarin's book has had only small circulation, Draco's true sweet nature may never be widely known, and the false myth of his harshness may endure. But not being a best-seller also has its advantages. It means, for instance, that *Drakon and Early Athenian Homicide Law* will not be included on the same book list that includes *My Turn* by Nancy Reagan (the former First Lady's memoir of her White House years) and *Drive* (the autobiography of Boston Celtic superstar Larry Bird).

February 14, 1990

Mr. Justice Zeus

He is probably a Democrat, because he is forever gathering the clouds. And he does not believe in the traditional family values, preferring to enjoy scores of affairs throughout Peloponnesia. Nonetheless Zeus is the most likely candidate to fill the next vacancy on the U.S. Supreme Court. What has caught the eye of the Justice Department is the way that Cronus' son can decide cases of life-and-death by pretending not to decide them, just as the Supreme Court did in *Whitmore v. Arkansas* (discussed below).

Pretending to be neutral, pretending to let the chips fall where they may, is one of Zeus' most accomplished strategies. In the fateful contest between Achilles and Hector (*The Iliad*, Book 22), Achilles attacked relentlessly, but Hector, protected by Apollo, always managed to escape unharmed. After the combatants had circled the fighting field of Troy four times, Zeus, apparently growing bored by the indecisive battle, ordained that the match should be resolved judicially. And so Zeus "balanced his golden scales, and in them set two fateful portions of death," one portion for Achilles and one portion for Hector.

At the beginning of the judicial process, both portions appeared to be in perfect balance; but very soon Hector's portion proved to be the heavier and it "dragged downward toward death." On all other occasions, when the scale is heavier on your side you win, but this time it was death that was being so precariously balanced, and so Hector, the breaker of horses, was doomed. Zeus, however, was always able to disclaim any responsibility, because all he did (he would explain) was to let fate decide; his golden scales (he would explain) were neutral. Zeus' disclaimer was, of course, a sham because without some protection from the gods Achilles (whose mother, Thetis, was a sea nymph) was certain to triumph over Hector (both of whose parents were mere mortals).

Disclaiming any responsibility for how the scales of justice tip is also the key to the Supreme Court's decision in the grim *Whitmore* case. That case involved one Ronald Gene Simmons who

> shot and killed two people and wounded three others in the course of a rampage through the town of Russellville. Arkansas. After police apprehended Simmons, they searched his home . . . and discovered the bodies of 14 members of Simmons' family, all of whom had been murdered.

Simmons was tried, convicted, and sentenced to death for both sets of murders. On each occasion, after being sentenced, Simmons stated formally that "it is my wish and my desire that absolutely no action by anybody be taken to appeal or in any way to change this sentence."

When Simmons refused to appeal, he aroused the interest of a fellow death row inmate, one Jonas Whitmore, who sought (as Simmons' "next friend") to appeal on his behalf. But the Supreme Court of Arkansas concluded that Whitmore had no legal standing, although it also acknowledged that there were "seven possible points that could be argued for reversal."

The question before the U.S. Supreme Court was whether, under the Constitution, Simmons' death sentence had to be reviewed by a higher Arkansas court if the only champion was the convict, Mr. Jonas Whitmore. The U.S. Supreme Court (by a vote of 7–2) made the technically correct, but morally indefensible, decision that the merits of the appeal were irrelevant. The only issue to be decided (held the Court) was whether Jonas Whitmore was a proper party to present the merits. Holding Whitmore to be "an intruder and uninvited meddler," the case was quickly dismissed and Simmons was (or will very soon be) executed. And no one will ever know whether any of those seven appellate points had merit, whether Simmons should have been executed.

But even if one of those appellate points had merit (was Simmons insane when he committed the murders, or when he renounced his right to appeal?), the Supreme Court has covered itself, because it had decided only the narrow innocent-sounding question of whether Whitmore was a proper party to bring the merits of the case to the Court's attention. And so the Supreme Court, like Zeus, disclaims responsibility for how the golden scales tip. And without the merits to ponder, *Whitmore* was decided with dispatch.

The ability to dissemble is not the only quality that Zeus would bring to the Supreme Court. He would be the first native-born Greek, giving that Court even greater diversity. And best of all, he'd bring his quiver of thunderbolts, so that cases henceforth could be decided more swiftly still, like lightning.

May 17, 1990

Does Odysseus Ride the 'A' Train?

Federal judges, none of whom ever changed trains at Columbus Circle, have written learned opinions on whether or not the government's recent ban on begging and panhandling in the subway is constitutional (*Young v. New York City Transit Authority*). Those opinions (which discuss, with erudition, whether begging is or is not free speech protected by the First Amendment) miss the point entirely (as one would expect from judges who never changed trains at Columbus Circle). The real point of the ban is that it is carefully and specifically limited to the subways; that means, in legal terms, that begging and panhandling are carefully and specifically *not* banned in stretch limos, on cruise ships and on the Concorde. (For those readers who are not lawyers: when interpreting a statute, things not specifically prohibited are, thereby, permitted; *expressio unius est exclusio alterius*.)

The government's action is in strict accord with the very latest legal thinking, which is that all laws should be based on economics; those laws are best which promote efficiency. Applying that principle to begging and panhandling, the government recognized that subway riders, as a group, are a parsimonious lot, so that soliciting alms from them was an inefficient use of a beggar's time. Studies showed that those few riders who contributed to passing tin (or paper) cups did so with pennies, nickels or dimes; the occasional rider who donated a quarter considered himself to be a philanthropist. But as our ever-alert government officials realized, the folks who shuffle around in stretch limos, on cruise ships and on the Concorde are big spenders, endowers of universities. Therefore, by shifting the beggars to them, great efficiency would be achieved. The average panhandler would probably collect more in a one-hour ride on those block-long off-white Cadillacs than he would in a whole week of travel on the "A" train. The only way that the stretch limo operators could divest themselves of the beggars—and perhaps they are too guilt-ridden even to try—would be to encourage the city to raise subway token prices significantly, perhaps to about $80 each, thereby attracting a ridership that might make panhandling in the subway once again worthwhile.

Odysseus returned home, disguised as a beggar, a "dismal vagabond" who "wore wretched clothing" (*Odyssey*, Book XVII, Richmond Lattimore translation). Most of the suitors treated him kindly. But Antinoos was cruel: "Do we not already have enough other vagabonds, and bothersome beggars to ruin our feasting?"

And finally, working himself into a fit, Antinoos struck the "wretched old man" with a footstool. The other suitors "were wildly indignant" at the attack for fear that the bothersome old man might be "some god from heaven."

For the gods do take on all sorts of transformation, appearing as strangers from elsewhere, and thus they range at large through the cities, watching to see which men keep the laws and which are violent.

I doubt that any of those toothless, armless, legless men who haunt the subways is the godlike Odysseus in disguise, for no make-up artist who ever lived could fashion such a change. But still, isn't it better to have them beg in the subway, where it never rains or snows and is never cold, than on the open, unprotected streets, streets that are already too clogged with all those block-long off-white stretch Cadillacs? Those stretch limos have an interesting feature other than their almost coast-to-coast size—their windows are one-way only (being opaque from the outside looking in and smoky from the inside looking out). So perhaps they're inhabited by judges who, seeing the problem through protective, murky glass, think that begging is an abstract question of free speech.

June 4, 1990

Lysistrata Dissents,
And Then Some

When she read what the five male Law Lords of the English House of Lords had held—

Marriage today is a partnership of equals—

Lysistrata couldn't stop laughing.

The facts that prompted the Lords' holding (i.e., that men and women were equal) were not unusual: A lorry driver and his wife had been estranged, and she left their home to live with her parents. After some three weeks of such separation, the husband forced his way into his in-law's home, and attempted, with force, to have relations with his wife. If they had not been married, the crime of attempted rape would have been clear. But at least since 1736 (when Sir Matthew Hale published his *History of the Pleas of the Crown*) it had been the law in England that a man could not be guilty of raping his wife because the right to sexual relations inhered in a marriage. It was the overturning of that 255-year-old precedent (by holding that a husband could be guilty of the crime of raping his wife) that made the House of Lords swell with the chivalrous pride of having given women equality, of having "brought the law into the 20th Century." But Lysistrata, as she had during the Peloponnesian War, voiced a different sentiment:

Women of Greece, just two and a half millennia ago we gathered here, at the Acropolis, to put an end to male violence and male arrogance. We each took a sacred oath to suffer no man's passion, be he husband or lover, until the male curbed his militant temper. And as Aristophanes has faithfully recorded, all praise to Athene, we triumphed. But we were naive in thinking that we had permanently subdued the male penchant for force, for sad it is that almost every rosy-fingered dawn brings us new reports of the male run amok with his muscles and weapons. Some males focus their violence against one woman, in rape; others continue in the way of Ares, warring wherever they can. But what I have said about the inferiority of the male is nothing new to us, for instead of using his brain he has always preferred to use his fist. I have summoned you here on this occasion, rousing you even from your marital beds, to report on a decision just handed down by five males in England's House of Lords. Note for the record, if you will, that it is not named the House of Ladies. And we note further for the record that unthinking male violence in England has been untrammeled for centuries: it is as widespread as the Aegean Sea and as turbulent as one of Poseidon's spiteful little storms. Although we women of Arcadia, by our stern resolve, ended all wars some 2,500 years ago, the Brits, who dwell west even of Iberia, have continued to practice that peculiar male sport. I don't want to bore you with a history lesson—I'll leave that to Herodotus—but English males roam the globe looking for wars, much as Agamemnon once did before we put a stop to it. English soldiers in the Crusades once wandered even to the most eastern shore of our own Mediterranean Sea; and there were two wars in far-away America; and there were continuous wars with France, from Agincourt to Waterloo. And once they found a war in South Africa, fighting the Boers. And then there were two world wars, where British soldiers left their families to march to every nook and cranny of the world. And just when things seemed quiet, when it seemed that British men had had enough of military pomp, troops were dispatched to the Falkland Islands, where even winged Mercury had never been. And not long ago, restless once more to put on armor, English battalions were sent to the Persian Gulf, unaware, apparently, that our braves soldiers had already defeated Xerxes at Thermopylae.

And so it is that the English male is still as violent as Achilles, still using his fist instead of his mind. But now to the point of this meeting: Using the slim pretext of one chariot driver's own individual violence—the despicable attempted rape of his wife—the highest court in England, using logic that would stir poor Aristotle from his grave, has gotten it all twisted by solemnly declaring that men are our equal. And so our purpose here is to urge our sisters in Albion to refuse to accommodate their husbands or lovers until the magistrates in England acknowledge, finally, as did the magistrates in Athens long ago, women's manifest superiority. We must do everything in our power to bring English law, even if kicking and screaming, into the 5th Century B.C.

November 8, 1991

Odysseus Never Used a Proxy

Odysseus visited the Underworld (*Odyssey*, Book XI), but it was not in connection with a shady stock manipulation. For shady stock manipulations take place right on the Earth's surface, in full view of everybody, especially of the United States Supreme Court.

Virginia Bankshares v. Sandberg, decided by the Supreme Court in June 1991, had these facts: One bank (First American Bankshares) owned 85 percent of another bank (Virginia Bankshares). But First American, like a spoiled child, wanted to own the whole thing, and so offered to pay, for each share it did not already have in its vault, $42.00. That offer was accompanied by a proxy statement that described the $42.00 price as "high" and as "fair." And based on that proxy statement representation of fairness, almost all of the minority stockholders tendered their shares. But the proxy statement was false. It was false because the stock was worth not $42.00 per share but $60.00, and so the United States Supreme Court found. From those set of facts one might deduce that the forced sellers of the Virginia Bankshares were awarded damages of $18.00 per share (being the difference between the $60.00 that the stock was worth and the $42.00 that they had been paid). But, despite that simple arithmetic, the Supreme Court held that the sellers were entitled to damages of zero.

The Court reasoned that since the liars owned 85 percent of Virginia Bankshares stock they had enough votes to force a merger at any price (and with any story, be that story be true or false). But not only was the Court's arithmetic (that $60.00 less $42.00 equals zero) faulty, but its legal analysis was worse. For despite the Supreme Court's argument to the contrary, had the proxy statement been true the $42.00 deal would not have taken place. For a true proxy statement would have stated: "Dear shareholders, Although your stock is worth $60.00 per share we are paying you only $42.00, because we already own 85 percent and there is nothing you can do about it except to be happy that we are not paying you $41.00 or maybe even $15.00 or how would you like $10.00, ha ha ha." It is certain that had the proxy statement told that truth the minority shareholders (1) would have either received the $60.00 per share to which they were entitled, or (2) there would have been no transaction. Indeed, the very reason for the falsehood was the knowledge that the truth would have torpedoed the deal.

The Court's theory, that wrongdoers could have done it legally anyway, could be a dangerous precedent. For instance, could a gunman who held up a store be able to argue for a reduced sentence on the ground that he didn't need the gun because he could have terrorized the little old sickly shopkeeper with only his bare fists? Will speeders now defend on the ground that they would have gotten to the very same place anyway had they gone more slowly? And what of the plagiarist who asserts that even if he had not read *Hamlet* he would have written the "To be or not to be" soliloquy because those were his very thoughts, exactly? Or the accused rapist who argues for acquittal because had he a little more time he would have convinced her?

When Odysseus visited his Mom in the Underworld he complained to her that he was "always suffering" because he so pined for his wife and home, for he had "wandered since the time [he] first went along with great Agamemnon to Ilion." But he very carefully did not tell her, as he described his meanderings, that he had spent seven years on the isle of Ogygia, where he had lived intimately with "the shining goddess," the beautiful Calypso. Nor did management tell the sellers that their stock was worth $60.00 per share. Both Odysseus and the bank management had a very good time doing the very same thing.

October 17, 1991

III
Judicial Logic,
Including
One Parody

A Stale
Slice of
the Law

"**R**emember Oliver Wendell Holmes' dissent in *Lochner*" is still not as evocative as "Remember the Alamo," but it is slowly getting there. In Judge Richard A. Posner's new book, *Law and Literature*, Holmes's dissent is rated as "merely the greatest judicial opinion of the last hundred years."

The thrust of this essay is to suggest that Holmes's beautifully written dissent is not the greatest opinion of this or any other century, but is, rather, weak, wrong and smug.

The facts in *Lochner v. New York* were these: In 1897 (before there was Wonder Bread and Pepperidge Farm croissants, i.e., when bread was made in small factories by hand) the New York State Legislature passed a law (sec. 110 of article 8, chapter 15) which provided that no bakery factory employee was allowed to work more than 60 hours a week or 10 hours a day. The law was prompted by findings that bakery employment was particularly hazardous.

The labor of the bakers is among the hardest and most laborious imaginable, because it has to be performed under conditions injurious to the health of those engaged in it. . . .

The constant inhaling of flour dust causes inflammation of the lungs and of the bronchial tubes. . . . The long hours of toil to which bakers are subject produce rheumatism, cramps and swollen legs. . . .

The average age of a baker is below that of other workmen; they seldom live over their fiftieth year, most of them dying between the ages of 40 and 50. During periods of epidemic diseases the bakers are generally the first to succumb to the disease, and the number swept away during such periods far exceeds the number of other crafts in comparison to the men employed in the respective industries.

Nonetheless, the United States Supreme Court (by a 5–4 vote) held that the New York bakery workers' protection statute was unconstitutional. The reasoning was that the Fourteenth Amendment, which guarantees our liberty, does not permit a state, willy-nilly, to interfere with the liberty of contract; if a baker's apprentice wants to work more than 10 hours a day or 60 hours a week and die, that (said the Supreme Court) was his constitutional right.

Three of the four dissenting justices joined in an opinion that, although written in legalese prose, hit the nail on the head: The New York law should be upheld (these three justices argued) because it "had appropriate and direct connection with that protection to life, health, and property which each State owes to her citizens." That simple, direct proposition seems to be unassailable.

A separate dissent, written by Mr. Justice Holmes in elegant prose, is the subject of this essay. On the wisdom of the New York statute enacted to protect bakery workers from dying young, the Holmes position was Olympian detachment. He stated that his own "agreement or disagreement" with the statute was irrelevant, and noted for the record that if he had to decide on the merits "I should desire to study it further and long before making up my mind." The crux of Holmes's opinion was that as long as some "reasonable man might think it a proper measure on the score of health," the law should be sustained whatever he, the judge, might think. It is that very detachment from the merits that has won the opinion-of-the-century recommendation from Judge Posner. But I suggest that Holmes's opinion would have been even more memorable had he shown a little fire, had he written something like this:

I don't have to study this issue for one more second. It is a perversion of our Constitution for the Supreme Court of the United States to invalidate a rational law that would save the lives and protect the health of thousands of vulnerable people.

But as bad (in this writer's opinion) as Holmes's aloof dissent is, the worst is still to come. There seems to be a movement afoot that argues that *Lochner* was rightly decided, and that the New York State law that protected the health and life of bakery workers *was* unconstitutional. Judge Posner writes (at p. 286 of his book): "After 82 years it is impossible to *prove* that *Lochner* was decided wrongly. The statute struck down in *Lochner* was paternalistic. . . ." A footnote (no. 21) on the same page records that "a growing scholarly movement regard it [*Lochner*] as having been decided correctly." We should note that the *Lochner* decision was overruled by the Supreme Court in the 1930s and had long been considered by many to be among the very worst decisions ever made; its threatened revival says something profound about the law's direction.

Pharaoh was offended by his baker and, in the imperial way of royal justice, sent him to jail. By chance, the baker was put into the same cell as Joseph, to whom he revealed his dream: He had balanced three white baskets on his head, and in the uppermost basket were bakemeats for Pharaoh, which the birds ate. Joseph interpreted that dream to mean that after three days the baker would be hanged. And so it came to pass, exactly as Joseph had foretold (Genesis, 40).

In justifying the Supreme Court's majority opinion in *Lochner* these conservative critics will undoubtedly argue that being harsh to bakers is not only constitutionally correct, but is part of our Judeo-Christian heritage.

October 14, 1988

A Roast
Leg of
Unicorn

If your local butcher went to his scale and carefully, meticulously weighed meat that didn't exist, perhaps a roast leg of unicorn, you would think he was daft. But just such a make-believe weigh-in has sent one Larry Youngblood of Tucson, Arizona, to jail.

The facts of the case (*Arizona v. Youngblood*), as set forth in a recent opinion of the U.S. Supreme Court, were these: A 10-year-old boy was sodomized on a Sunday evening after church and he identified one Larry Youngblood as his attacker; Youngblood protested his innocence. The only evidence at the trial, one way or the other, was the boy's identification. Whether it was accurate or not we will never know, but of one thing we can be sure: however hesitant or tentative that first recognition may have been, it necessarily (if inadvertently) became unshakable as the trial continued; for every day the victim would see the accused, looking meaner and meaner, huddled with his lawyer at the defense table. "He's the one. I'm positive."

Youngblood's only hope was to demonstrate that the semen stains that the police had found on the boy's T-shirt were not his; those stains, when analyzed by forensic chemists, would prove, beyond doubt, his innocence or guilt. But, alas, the police had negligently forgotten to refrigerate the shirt, and so the dispositive evidence was lost forever. The jury, nonetheless, convicted. The Supreme Court of Arizona reversed on the ground that police negligence had deprived the defendant of a fair trial. But the Supreme Court of the United States had no such doubt, and the conviction was reinstated (three justices dissenting).

The key point is the trial judge's charge to the jury: "If you find that the state has . . . allowed to be destroyed or lost any evidence whose content or quality are in issue, you may infer that the true fact is against the state's interest." Since their verdict was "guilty as charged," the jury necessarily found that there was no "issue" concerning the "content" of the stain. It is miraculous that they could have reached any conclusion, since there was no stain to evaluate.

What kind of scale does a jury use to weigh evidence that doesn't exist? Is it one of those balance scales used in candy stores, with the little weights on one side and dried apricots (my favorite) on the other? Or one of those new-fangled electronic scales, where the weight and price per ounce are automatically multiplied digitally in lights before your very eyes? Or is it a gauge of the mind, calibrated at the factory to measure, in kilograms, only things imaginary? Or perhaps it is a scale of the heart that registers, according to Jerome Kern, whenever smoke gets in your eyes; or a scale of the passions, similar to the device used at the trial of Sacco and Vanzetti. That one happens to be the most popular and most durable model ever built, and has been in service here and abroad, over the centuries, in thousands of cases.

But whatever measure the jury used, and the Supreme Court sanctioned, it should be patented. The proceeds from the licensing fees would retire the national debt before George Bush submitted his first budget. The marketing people would advertise it as the Opposite Scale, or the Upside Down Scale, or perhaps, more simply, the Reverse Scale, for it would be the only scale in the world on which nothing outweighed everything. The commercial possibilities are limitless: heavy folks would buy one, and no longer suffer a diet of carrots and cauliflower; millions of potential astronauts would use them to experience all the sensations of a weightless moon-walk without the risk of rocket failure; and concrete manufacturers would use them to ship tons of their product around the globe for a few cents. Of course carriers, like railroads and postmen, would be less enthusiastic. But, as courts frequently note, the balance of justice cannot always be perfect.

By using the Reverse Scale, the *Youngblood* case got everything backwards. The negligent Tucson police forgot to refrigerate one boy's stained T-shirt and so, to make up for it, they put one Larry Youngblood in the cooler.

January 11, 1989

The
Peppered
Moth

The peppered moth is "a striking example of evolution
in action," one of the most dramatic proofs of Charles
Darwin's theory of natural selection. (The quotation
is from Richard E. Leakey's *Introduction to the Illustrated Origin of Species*.) That same moth is also (at least in this essay) a metaphor for the
law.

The peppered moth was once silver-colored. When it clung to a
lichen-covered tree bark its camouflage was so perfect that hungry birds
flew by but never noticed it. Then came the Industrial Revolution, and
its soot killed the lichen and blackened the tree trunks. Soon—and
"soon" means a few dozen years—the black mutant version of the peppered moth began to dominate the forest because, with its perfect camouflage, only it escaped its predators.

The laws of nature (as described by Darwin) and the laws of man (as
described in many books on jurisprudence) have developed by the same
process. Both begin with a model—a plant or animal in nature, a precedent in the law—and evolve over time. Sometimes changes are slow.
For instance (in nature) the insects that annoy us every summer began
in the palaeozoic era, some 400 million years ago; and (in law) capital
punishment is recorded in the Bible. But when the environment changes

suddenly, evolution responds swiftly. It is always interesting to examine how one model in nature or one precedent in the law develops into its successor.

And so we focus our microscope on *California v. Trombetta,* one of the most routine, uninteresting cases ever decided by the U.S. Supreme Court. The question was whether the actual, physical breath samples exhaled by an arrested drunk driver had to be preserved for the trial or whether, instead, the printout record of the Omicron Intoxilyzer (the machine that measures the alcoholic content of one's breath) was sufficient evidence. Since the accuracy of the Intoxilyzer was conceded—and since, therefore, there was no doubt about what the evidence was—the conviction was unanimously upheld.

Although *Trombetta* (decided in 1984) is not very interesting as a case, it is fascinating as a precedent. It was cited and relied on by the Supreme Court majority in *Arizona v. Youngblood,* decided in 1988. In *Youngblood,* the defendant was convicted of sodomy on the testimony of the victim, a 10-year-old boy. The Tucson police had negligently failed to refrigerate the boy's T-shirt, which had semen samples that would have established, dispositively, Youngblood's guilt or innocence. Because he had been denied the opportunity to establish his innocence, the Supreme Court of Arizona held that Youngblood had been denied a fair trial, and it reversed his conviction.

But the U.S. Supreme Court, by a 6–3 vote, reinstated the jury's verdict of guilty. In doing so—and that is the point of this essay—the Court cited and relied on *Trombetta* as the controlling precedent. Since *Trombetta* had held that all physical evidence need not be preserved for the trial, the *Youngblood* majority concluded that, therefore, the police's "failure to preserve potentially useful evidence does not constitute a denial of due process of law."

And so the U.S. Supreme Court, like the peppered moth, went from white to black in record time. *Trombetta* had held that physical evidence did not have to be retained *because* there was an unchallenged record of precisely what that evidence was. *Youngblood* held the opposite—that physical evidence need not be retained even though there was *no* way of knowing what that destroyed evidence would prove. Although standing for opposite propositions, the amazing thing is that *Youngblood* cites *Trombetta* as its binding precedent.

Although evolution in nature and evolution in law have similar characteristics, there should be one big difference: Improvement of a species in nature refers only to its ability to survive; the silver moth and the black moth, each clinging tenaciously to the tree trunk, enjoy the same quality of life. But improvement in the law is supposed to do more; it is supposed to make things better. That is why comparing the *Youngblood* opinion to the peppered moth may be so unflattering. But, sadly, the resemblance is there: that opinion so camouflages the governing precedent (*Trombetta*) that the law has become invisible.

February 14, 1989

The Case of
the Unexplained
Differential

I had never before seen Holmes so perplexed. For several days he had been studying a crate of documents that had been sent by special courier from America. All that I knew about them was that the large box in which they were delivered bore the legend: "*Sharif v. New York State Education Department,* 88 Civ. 8435, U.S. District Court, Southern District of New York."

Holmes tapped his fingers on the table as he read and reread every sheet of paper, some under his lens. After several pensive moments, he turned to me and said, "Watson, this is not only a baffling case, but a delicate one. May I explain it to you?" Since I was most eager to discover what it was that so troubled my friend, I urged him to tell me all without delay.

"In order to qualify for college, most American high school students are required to take a two-part examination called the Scholastic Aptitude Test, known to all as the SATs. One part tests English skills and the other part tests mathematical skills. This standardized test is important because there is such a wide range of quality among American high schools that colleges need some objective way to evaluate candidates for admission."

"It makes perfect sense to me," I interjected.

"But that is only the beginning of this case, Watson. The State of New York, to save money, uses the results of the SATs to award scholarships."

"That seems democratic," I observed. "That way all of those scholarships are awarded on merit and there can be no charge of favoritism. I suggest that we employ the same system here in England." I detected a slight smile when Holmes replied that not everybody saw it that way. That startled me, because I could not see who could find fault with a system that was based solely on merit.

Observing my bewilderment, Holmes resumed his explanation.

"The two test components, the English and the mathematics, are graded separately. The results are then added together, and the persons with the highest total scores are awarded the scholarships, called Regent Scholarships. The focus of our problem is in the mathematics examination. It appears that every year the boys as a group outscore the girls as a group very substantially, always by about 40 points. For example, in 1988 the mean score on the mathematics test for the boys was 498, but it was only 455 for girls. As a result of that variation, the boys win over 70 percent of the scholarships every year, although they comprise slightly less than 50 percent of the total number of children taking the SATs."

As his story was unfolding I interrupted to ask my friend why the papers he was studying so carefully were boxed in a container bearing the strange legend set forth above. Holmes, his brow furrowed, went on to recount the strange reason.

In America, it appears, people who are dissatisfied with almost anything tend to institute a lawsuit. In this instance a group of high school girls, aware that they would not score well enough on the mathematics examination to qualify for a Regent Scholarship, sued to enjoin the New York State Education Department from awarding those scholarships on the basis of the SATs. They alleged that the mathematics examination discriminated against their sex, hence violated the American Constitution. And most amazing of all, at least to myself who is not very learned in the ways of the American legal system, the judge agreed. After studying the matter for several weeks, the court concluded that the reason for the point differential "remains unexplained." And since he found that there was no rational explanation for the disparity of results, he concluded, as only judges can, that therefore the mathematics component of the SATs must be discriminatory.

Holmes, of course, enjoys a worldwide reputation for being able to find the proper explanation for almost any problem. To him, there is no such thing as a riddle that "remains unexplained." And so he was retained—he would not disclose the identity of his client even to me—to see if there was, indeed, some rational explanation for the gap in scores. The matter was delicate because if Holmes did find an explanation, it might tend to show that the judge had not been as careful as he might have been. But, of course, Holmes has faced that same dilemma with Scotland Yard many times over the years, and it has never once deterred him.

Holmes returned all the papers to the box, exactly in the order as they had been delivered, and announced that he thought he had found the solution. I was quite amazed at his speed, since he had the documents for only four days.

"I've not been idle," he remarked with his customary understatement. "But at first I did take several false steps that almost led me far astray. I noted, at the start of my inquiry, that the mathematics score differential between the boys group and the girls group corresponded almost exactly to the groups' respective size differential. That is, the average 17-year-old boy is both taller and heavier than the average 17-year-old girl in about the very ratio that boys score better than girls in the math SAT. The statistical parallel is so striking that for several days I was convinced that that was the solution. But then I noted that Asian-Americans, the smallest of test-takers physically, have achieved the highest scores. Therefore, there is no correlation between a person's size and his or her mathematical ability."

I marveled at the way Holmes was willing—almost eager—to disprove his own theory. I have observed that most people do the opposite; once they have reached a conclusion they bend the facts to support it. That is why Holmes is so extraordinary.

Just then there was a knock on the door, and a messenger with a large book entitled *Schwann* was ushered into the room. My friend thanked the young man, and suggested to me that he may now have the corroboration to prove his theory. Holmes explained that the catalogue contained every available compact disc and record alphabetized by composer, from Aaquist Johansen to Zyman. After studying the catalogue, which is about the size of one London telephone book, Holmes announced that, despite the judge's finding to the contrary, there was, indeed, an explanation for that 40-point differential in math scores between boys and girls. I wondered again at his amazing power to bring order where there had been confusion, to explain things that are inexplicable to the rest of us.

"Let me begin with the corroborating evidence first, Watson, then we'll get to the proof itself. There is, you know, a very high correlation between the ability to compose music and the ability to solve theoretical mathematical problems. Mozart and Bach, had they been so inclined, would have been wonderful astronomers. As you know Watson, I myself dabble in both musical composition and algebraic theory. A study of this comprehensive *Schwann* catalogue confirms that over the centuries and until this very day virtually every single composer of serious classical music has been a male."

I confessed that I was stunned by his statement, but I had to concede that I could cite no exception.

"The catalogue only confirms what I had already deduced independently from the data contained in the court file. The reason that boy high school seniors as a group always outscore girls as a group can be explained by this elementary fact, which somehow eluded the court. Boys are better mathematicians than girls."

After stating his solution, which I could not contravene, Holmes became quite philosophical as he wondered aloud why so obvious a conclusion had not occurred to the court in New York. As he mulled the reasons, he conjectured that people had become so sensitive about equality that they had trouble recognizing that one group may be better in a particular skill than another. He noted, for instance, that we English were better cricket players than the Americans, but that did not make us better athletes. Similarly, he suggested, the fact that boys were better in geometry than girls did not make them smarter or wiser. As he ended his ruminations I thought that I detected a rare smile when he said that he hoped that the courts would not enjoin the playing of Beethoven's Violin Concerto, one of his favorites, because some judge could not explain why it was that all serious music has been composed by males.

March 23, 1989

The Law and the Yucca Yucca Plant

A rather routine speech by Chief Justice Rehnquist before a rather routine audience (the Brookings Institution) has mushroomed into one of the most important legal events of the century. Commenting on the growth of litigation under the Racketeer Influenced and Corrupt Organizations Law (popularly known as RICO), the Chief Justice stated (twice) that "garden variety" crimes did not belong in the federal court. Seedless to say, defense attorneys, ever alert, began making hay at once. Within seconds they filed dozens of botanical motions to dismiss the cases pending against their clients. Lawyers for the nation's leading mobsters argued that they had to be freed because each was a perfect example of that most common of Honduran garden varieties, a top banana; the plea on behalf of underlings was that their exoneration was required precisely because they were, like that most common of Maine's plants, small potatoes. Tax claims were challenged on the furrowed ground that it was no longer necessary to pay lettuce to the IRS. An alleged murderer in the *Arsenic and Old Lace* mold was freed after she told authorities where she had berried her victims. A judgment that had been rendered for riparian damage was reversed because matters involving currants were no longer cognizable in the federal courts. One armed robbery conviction was set aside when the alleged perpetrator proved in open court that he had been stalked by the FBI. Every day the bar invented new ways to beet the rap. Thus, all federal liens were released because, it was argued, no assets could be cucumbered; and subpoenas of every kind were squashed. Sometimes, however, judges eager to curry favor with the Boss went too far. For instance, one hard-of-hearing inexperienced magistrate in North Dakota barred appearances by all Spanish-speaking lawyers in the mistaken belief that they were included in the Chief Justice's ban on avocados. When told that his speech was causing chaos, the Chief merely shrubbed his shoulders. Defense lawyers could not recall a better frond.

Legal scholars, who parse-nipped every word of Mr. Rehnquist's remarks, began to realize that every crime was of the "garden variety," because every kind of heist, murder, or scam had been attempted thousands and thousands of times before. It was concluded, therefore, that if "garden variety" offenses were excluded from the court's docket, no crimes at all would be left to try. And if "garden variety" civil cases were also deleted—and that seemed to be the Chief's direction—there would be absolutely nothing for federal judges to do. And that analysis made old-time lawyers and judges fret that perhaps they had devoted their careers—their lives—to a "garden variety" profession. Some of those veterans began to worry that since the law was based on precedent (and the older the better), new and creative ideas might be outside the legal profession almost by definition. Practicing law was not like painting a picture or composing an opera, and certainly not like writing an essay.

As for the Chief Justice's speech, a more earthy interpretation was that it was given in response to the Congress's refusal to enact the judicial pay raise bill. What the Chief was saying was that federal judges would simply refuse to conduct any more trials until Congress raised their celery.

June 16, 1989

A Practical
Solution to
Birmingham's
Dilemma

T*he Skin of Our Teeth,* by Thornton Wilder (1942), is a
play about keeping the fires burning; *Martin v. Wilks,*
by Chief Justice Rehnquist (1989), is a 5–4 opinion
about putting the fires out. This essay connects them, both metaphorically and arithmetically.

The Skin of Our Teeth is a comedy about Mankind's struggle, since the
Creation, to make progress; included in the cast are cameo roles for Homer, Moses, a dinosaur and a mammoth. The Ice Age has set in (is it a
new primordial freeze or the same old cold that chilled our ancestors?),
and Mr. George Antrobus, a commuter from New Jersey, is trying to
keep warm while he creates our civilization. Although it is August, all
of his chairs and books have been readied for the fireplace; only the
Shakespeares are being spared. Despite the adverse weather conditions,
Mr. Antrobus is not a quitter. After 5,000 diligent years he had invented
both the wheel and the alphabet. But of particular importance for this
essay, he has also begun to work on some basic rules of arithmetic. As
the play ends, the ice has begun to recede, and there is an undercurrent
of sentimental optimism that maybe, this time, the world will really be-

come a better, a more inhabitable place. Of course 1942, for those too young to know or remember, was one of the low points of Western Civilization—the Axis armies were on the march—and any flicker of hope, even if only from a playwright, was greatly appreciated.

But the denouement of Act III was, to some, just theater. For proof that the Ice Age never melted, we note, for instance, that in 1974 it was proven in federal court that the Birmingham Alabama Fire Department did not, as a matter of policy, hire blacks. A lawsuit was brought under Title VII of the Civil Rights Act, and Birmingham was forced, by a settlement, to hire and promote blacks in the future. That settlement was embodied in a formal document called a Consent Decree, which was signed by the parties and "So Ordered" by the judge. Subsequently, a group of white firefighters brought their own suit—*Martin v. Wilks*—alleging that that very Decree, by establishing a formula for hiring and promoting blacks, violated *their* rights under Title VII. Since it was obvious that if the Birmingham Fire Department was required to hire and promote more blacks, it would, as a matter of arithmetic, necessarily be hiring and promoting fewer whites, no one paid too much attention to the *Martin* litigation. But as Thornton Wilder observed, Ice Ages and dinosaurs linger, and in that spirit, the United States Supreme Court held, 5–4, that just because the Birmingham Fire Department had been required to hire and promote more blacks did *not* mean that it could, ipse dixit, hire and promote fewer whites.

At first blush, the High Court's decision seemed to pose an impossible dilemma, a mathematical paradox that defied solution. Just when even the logicians had despaired, George Antrobus, the inventor of the wheel and the alphabet, offered a solution. And a dazzling solution it was, made the more brilliant for its simplicity. He was in his garage tinkering with the basic rules of arithmetic when the answer almost presented itself. He recalled how, when working on the alphabet, he had varied the order of the letters many times before finally settling on the sequence of A, B, C, etc. through Z. Similarly, he now proposed, before he etched them in granite, to change the order of digits so that "5" would be smaller than "4." Thus the progression would be very slightly altered—no one would even notice—to 1, 2, 3, 5, 4, 6, 7, 8, 9. Hence Mr. Rehnquist's five-vote opinion in *Martin* would be the dissent, and Mr. Justice Stevens's four-vote opinion would be the law. And so it was, and the Birmingham Fire Department's crisis neatly disappeared.

There were, to be sure, some side effects. Since all other 5–4 Supreme Court decisions were similarly undone, many law review articles had to be recast. But those legal problems were simple compared to baseball's: Since all won-and-lost records of all major league teams had to be re-computed to reflect the new values of 5 and 4, the standings, since 1900, had to be adjusted accordingly. Where necessary, new pennant winners had to be given the opportunity to play in the World Series. The record books will have a lot of asterisks.

The Commissioner of Baseball agreed with civil rights advocates—it was well that this session of the Supreme Court had finally ended.

July 5, 1989

Of Seamen
and Bartenders

The justices of the U.S. Supreme Court could finish any crossword puzzle, even those impossibly hard ones that appear in British literary magazines, in seconds. The judges' secret is not in mastering the Oxford Unabridged Dictionary; their secret, rather, is being able to define, by fiat, any word in any way they want. For instance, in *McDermott International v. Jon C. Wilander* (decided in February 1991), the Court held, unanimously, that the word "seaman" applied to all employees aboard a ship, including such disparate types as carpenters, cooks, engineers, firemen, painters, cabin boys, coopers, waiters, surgeons, and even bartenders. The reason for the Court's expansive definition is that Congress (in 1920) passed a law, the Jones Act, the purpose of which was to protect seamen injured in the course of their employment. The law has always regarded mariners with special solicitude, because landlubber legislators seem to regard the sea as always raging and stormy, so that helpless men need all the protection, however meager, that legislators can bestow. Perhaps the lawmakers' concern began with their remembering, as children in Sunday School, the Book of Jonah, when "the Lord sent out a great wind into the sea, and there was a mighty tempest in the sea, so that the ship was like to be broken. Then the mariners were afraid . . ." (Chap. I, verses 4 and 5). Or perhaps they had seen pictures of Winslow Homer's *Nor-*

theaster or *Gulf Stream* (with sharks as well as a storm). Although the reason for stretching the definition of "seaman" to include even Jon C. Wilander, a sandblaster and painter, is understandable, the Court's lexicographical maneuver—inventing a definition to suit the need—is a precedent that has far-reaching implications.

The central issue when the President vetoed the Civil Rights Act of 1990 was whether the bill, as enacted, required quotas: Would blacks, Hispanics, Asians, women, gays and leprechauns have some legal advantage in job applications? Had the matter been argued before it, the Court could have resolved the question simply by redefining "minority" to include Caucasian males (who are, to be sure, a minority in the world). With their own employment thus legislatively protected, the Occidental ethnic crowd would have supported the Civil Rights Act of '90, which then would have been passed by the Congress unanimously and would have been signed by the President with a flourish. And the nation would have been spared a divisive debate.

Another touchy issue—can the nation march to war without a formal Congressional declaration of war (which appears to be required by Article I, Sec. 8 of the Constitution)—can also be resolved by a mere definition. All that the Supreme Court would have to do is define the term "war" as excluding a conflict in which Baghdad is bombed, or in which only 540,000 troops, albeit in full regalia, are sent overseas.

But the art of redefining is not limited to resolving questions of great national moment. The technique can also be used for personal matters of some delicacy. For instance, when Odysseus read the *McDermott International* opinion he had an idea, an inspiration. If one Jon Wilander, a mere sandblaster and painter, could be held to be a "seaman" (and hence come under the protection of the Jones Act), surely he, the finest mortal mariner and navigator in all Ithaca, was a person protected by that magic law. And since Poseidon's wrath had caused him to be shipwrecked, he could surely state a proper claim for relief for his anguish. For years he had struggled in vain to return to his dear and faithful wife Penelope and to his native island. For her part, each night Penelope would unravel her weaving, for she had promised to marry one of the suitors as soon as she finished the afghan; and as she secretly unraveled the thread in the wee hours, she pined for her loyal mate, who was marooned on some distant island far from home, if alive at all.

Although the "resourceful Odysseus" was also pining, marooned as he was on a distant island far from home, he was, in addition, able to do some unwinding of his own. Every night, in the inner recess of a hollowed cave, he and "the shining goddess," "the queenly nymph" Calypso, "enjoyed themselves in love." While back in the pre-feminist days of the Trojan War a double standard might be tolerated, the Odysseus of 1991 needed a new definition of "adultery" to calm his conscience, if not his good and faithful wife's anger. A simple, straightforward solution, in the spirit of *McDermott International,* was soon at hand. "Adultery" would, henceforth, be defined to exclude an affair with a goddess. Everyman, following the precedent of the godlike Odysseus, would be free to have a romance beyond his wife, provided only that the object of his affections was, truly, a goddess. Since it involves a subjective standard, who is and who is not a goddess is a question that is not always easy to answer. Which is why there are those who feel that the U.S. Supreme Court is better at solving crossword puzzles than legal issues.

March 15, 1991

A Concise History of Haberdashery and the Law

Despite the impeccable logic of his briefs and the soaring rhetoric of his oral arguments, Aristotle had never won a case. He pondered that apparent inconsistency, and as he espadrilled about Athens he suddenly thought of the solution. Judges, he concluded, don't weigh what you say as much as they weigh who you are. Satisfied that he had solved the problem, Aristotle donned his rich gold chain, from which he ostentatiously hung a button with the likeness of his student and patron, Alexander the Great (as faithfully depicted in Rembrandt's "Aristotle Contemplating the Bust of Homer," which hangs in New York's Metropolitan Museum of Art). Thenceforth, Aristotle never lost a decision.

Aristotle's incisive thinking has been followed until this very day, and not only by students of classical Greece. Lawyers who don't know Helen of Troy from Helena, Montana, know that those who wear button-down collars and three-button suits—buttons only slightly more subtle than the likeness of Alexander the Great—are far more likely to win their cases, for challenging the buttons of authority is not what judges often do.

But wear a "Ready to Strike" button, as one Legal Aid lawyer recently did (conveying the idea that if labor negotiations were not successful a walkout would follow), and the judges pounce. The trial judge (there was no jury involved) ruled that the button "politicized" an "extraneous" issue, and banned it in his courtroom. On appeal, the ban was reversed (one judge dissenting) on the Constitutional ground of free speech. (The case is reported as *Frankel v. Roberts*.)

Despite what the trial judge held, "extraneous" symbols have always been the stuff of the law. Before I learned of the commanding legal significance of buttons, I learned about the importance of another haberdashery item—hats. I remember the requirement, when I was in my last year of law school, that those who were invited to be interviewed by the great law firm of Davis Polk & Wardwell were expected to wear a bonnet. That headdress *sine qua non* was not strictly enforced for preliminary campus interviews, but those few who survived that first early round and were invited to visit the firm's New York office were politely advised of the topper that was expected. I must note that I myself was never interviewed by that firm, either on campus or off, so that this paragraph is just a musing from afar. But I did wonder at the time what the reason was for the stovepipe requirement, and how it was related to the law. I had often heard from Mom, because I never wore a hat, even in the winter, unless it rained, that I would always be cold because 80 percent of your body heat escaped through the top of your head. So I wondered, in my last year of law school, whether a bowler, winter or summer, might not also help you retain 80 percent of your ideas. Perhaps that is why, I thought, firms like Davis Polk & Wardwell were so successful; it just might be, I thought, that their competitors' ideas simply escaped through their partners' thinning hair into the ionosphere. More than one classmate mused at Davis Polk's insistence on a hat—it was, I note, a typical requirement in those years for the so-called white-shoe firms of Wall Street—because Mr. John W. Davis of Davis Polk had been the lead counsel in the landmark case of *Brown v. Board of Education*, lead counsel, that is, in favor of continued segregation. To some sourgrapers like myself—for chapeau or not, Davis Polk wasn't hiring me—the insistence on a fedora while at the same time, defending segregation did seem like a confusion of form and substance, like putting a rich Swiss chocolate topping on a scoop of tasteless vanilla ice milk.

We can all summon the picture of the criminal who is the "experienced Legal Aid client." We see him every night on the television news—a bedraggled fellow who wears neither button-down collars nor a homburg. But does his dress really matter to the law in 1991? One issue in *Frankel v. Roberts* was whether wearing a "Ready to Strike" button would affect the sacred attorney-client relationship because it might make the Legal Aid clients fearful of being abandoned by their court-appointed counselors. One appellate judge (who agreed that the lower court's ban of the "Strike" button was unconstitutional) addressed the attorney-client relationship issue and concluded, contrary to the opinion of the trial judge, that the wearing of such a button would make "the experienced" Legal Aid criminal defendant joyous

> . . . holding out, as it does, the prospect of a strike which hopefully would serve to postpone the day of reckoning in his case. Delay in a criminal case, as such a client knows, plays into his hands far more frequently than those of the People.

Aristotle, in the *Prior Analytics* and the *Posterior Analytics,* is credited with having invented the syllogism. Applying Aristotle's logic to the concurring opinion in *Frankel v. Roberts* results in the following sequence:

Every man is presumed innocent.

Every presumed innocent man would want his trial to be held speedily so that his innocence could be established speedily.

Therefore: Judges who state before trial that a defendant prefers a delay must necessarily presume that man to be guilty.

It is sad to see how one criminal defendant's dishabille—his lack of a button-down collar and a homburg—can so quickly undress the Constitution.

April 22, 1991

A Signal
Defiance

The Supreme Court ruled in *Rust v. Sullivan* that federally funded agencies could not discuss abortion. When it read *Rust*, the Justice Department promptly brought suit against the very same Supreme Court because, being a federally funded agency, the Court was thereby itself precluded from discussing abortion. A pretty neat little lawsuit, thought the Attorney General; and an airtight one, too. The nine justices were reportedly poring over the many texts and statutes in their law library, groping for a response. But the two best arguments that the judges and their clerks could muster—that the Justice Department's lawsuit violated the Court's First Amendment right of free speech, and that the government's suit had interfered with the Court's ability to function in the very area of its own expertise—were both arguments that the Court itself had summarily rejected in *Rust*.

As the stunned defendants sat around their famous table, a nervous Chief Justice asked for suggestions. One judge opined that the Court could sidestep the *Rust* ban by ignoring the word "abortion" and using, instead, the French word "*avortement*." The judges were gleeful that such a direct solution had been found, for a rereading of *Rust* demonstrated that that decision contained no restriction on discussing *avortement* or anything foreign.

But then, as sometimes happens in the law, there was a second thought. What, for instance, if a poor pregnant Parisian girl were to read the opinion with the *avortement* word; would not *she* consider the text to be a discussion of abortion, the very subject matter outlawed by *Rust*? There was gloom again, when suddenly another solution was proposed. Since *Rust* was to be strictly construed (all nine justices agreed on that), the way around it was for the Court, in all future opinions, to spell "abortion" phonetically, because *Rust* had said nothing—absolutely nothing—about "aborshun." An analysis of *Rust* confirmed that finding, and the Court's despair lifted once more, for a workable answer to the government's lawsuit seemed to have been found after all. But then, as sometimes happens in the law, someone thought about the new idea for just a moment, and then cautiously suggested that a mere rearrangement of letters would not avoid the spirit of *Rust,* which prohibited any discussion of "abortion" without regard to any particular spelling. The Court became dour again as it pondered its quagmire. Then a sudden burst of hope, as another justice, in a small, tentative voice, whispered that he had just thought of a possible countermove. Rather than using the *word* "abortion," however spelled, the Court could use, instead, the Morse code equivalent, for surely there was nothing in *Rust* that precluded even a federally funded agency from using an assortment of dots and dashes. That idea gained favor quickly, for it was noted that only telegraph operators would understand what was being reported, and the Court could always ask the Congress to pass a law forbidding poor pregnant women from being telegraph operators. Making it illegal for poor pregnant women to be telegraph operators made sense, agreed all the black robed ones, because using their fingers like that all the time could injure the fetus.

But dots and dashes, dashes and dots clacking over the wires was too noisy for the law, and when law libraries began to vibrate every time the Supreme Court discussed abortion, a new and more quiet rebuttal had to be found, one that did not call staccato attention to the very topic that, legally, had to be shunned.

When another defendant said that he hoped that there would be an admirable retort, the problem was suddenly solved: the Supreme Court, whenever it discussed abortion, would use semaphore banners. It was noiseless; and since it could be observed only by those with high-resolution binoculars, few, if any, poor pregnant women would ever know about it. And better still, the Justice Department, despite its electronic listening devices, would never learn that the Supreme Court, a federally funded agency, was discussing abortion in violation of its own ruling in *Rust v. Sullivan.*

Despite harsh criticism from strict constructionists, the High Court continued to discuss abortion by semaphore signals. It demonstrated, said the Court, that its devotion to women's rights was unflagging.

~ *June 12, 1991*

Perhaps

The *Killer,* a three-act play by Eugene Ionesco (first performed in 1957), is about random murders. *Hadley v. Baxendale,* an English case (decided in 1854), is about contract law. *Hadley v. Baxendale* is the scarier.

As the final curtain falls, Berenger, the principal character in *The Killer,* moans a fatalistic moan:

> "Oh God! There's nothing we can do. What can we do . . . what can we do . . ."

A killer has stalked the neighborhood, and even though clues to his identity and violent plans have become known, Berenger's attempts to stop the murders and arrest the culprit are bogged down in official indifference. And soon even Berenger himself is infected by the casualness; as he heads toward the Prefecture to report the new facts he begins to waver:

> "Perhaps the murderer will strike again tonight . . . I've simply got to stop him. I *must* go. I'm going. [Another two or three paces in the direction of the supposed Prefecture:] Come to think of it, it's all the same really, as it's too late. Another victim here or there, what's it matter in the state we're in . . . We'll go tomorrow, go tomorrow, Edouard and I, and much simpler that way, the offices will be closed this evening, perhaps they are already . . . What good would it do to . . ."

And in the end Berenger, too, becomes a victim, because nothing, not even murder, seems to matter.

The Killer was written to pose profound questions of philosophy, questions that ask why we are here and who we are and how we should conduct ourselves. But *Hadley v. Baxendale,* reported at 156 English Reports 145 (1854), is merely a legal opinion, albeit a landmark one, on contract law. Contract law is a subject that is usually duller than one of those black-on-black pictures (by Ad Reinhardt) that sometimes hang in the Museum of Modern Art. Despite its contract law provenance, *Hadley* is premised on, amid its typical legalese, amazing logic. It is the same nothing-matters logic that drives *The Killer.*

The facts in *Hadley* were these: A mill in Gloucester stopped working because its crank shaft broke. That broken shaft had to be shipped to the manufacturer, Joyce & Co., in Greenwich, for repair, and it was entrusted to the well-known common carrier, Pickford & Co. But because of Pickford & Co.'s negligence—it did not, apparently, run the tightest ship in the shipping business—the delivery of the broken shaft was delayed. And delayed, too, of course, was its repair. And as those dominoes fell, the mill's reopening was similarly postponed, whereupon the mill owners sued the shipping company for the profits they thereby lost. The lower court judge, Judge Crompton of the Gloucester Assizes, finding plaintiff's case to be compelling (as do I), awarded the miller damages of 25 pounds.

But the appellate court, in a burst of existentialist theater-of-the-absurd logic, rather rare for 1854, reversed. The errant shipper was not liable for the lost profits, reasoned the higher court, because it did not know that the broken crank shaft (that it was all-too-slowly carrying to Greenwich) was needed to make the mill operate. Perhaps, wrote Judge Ionesco—no, it was Judge Alderson—the mill had a spare crank shaft (perhaps in its cellar or attic or in some old bin where it kept the spare tires and obsolete computer terminals). Or perhaps (this is still either the playwright or the jurist) another vital piece of mill machinery had broken at the exact instant that the crank shaft broke, so that fixing the crank shaft would still not make the mill work. Concluding that the shipper could have no inkling that the broken crank shaft entrusted to it was needed to turn the wheels of the mill, the appellate court held that it was not liable for the delay admittedly caused by its own negligence.

Nothing matters. Perhaps the Prefecture is closed anyway (so there is no point to rushing there). Perhaps the mill could have operated without the broken crank shaft. And perhaps the mill may not have operated even had the shaft been fixed. Each "perhaps" is absurd. The difference is— and that is why *Hadley v. Baxendale* is so scary—that only the playwright meant it to be that way.

December 20, 1991

IV
Judges—How They
Got There and
Plan to Stay

Tying the Judicial Knot

J udges become judges, not through spontaneous genera-
tion (although sometimes the results seem just that random), but through one of two political routes. Either
they must run in an election (as do New York State judges) or they are
appointed by the chief executive (as are federal judges). Since the candidates elected to New York State judgeships, at least as those vigorous
campaigns are waged in New York City, are the candidates who are best
able to afford lavish advertising, including, specifically, placing their
posters in the advertising space carried on the outside of buses, some
critics have suggested that there is a lack of dignity in our local judicial
selection process.

That alleged lack of dignity is underscored, perhaps, by the fact that
when there is not a judicial election going on, that same bus advertising
space usually carries an ad for designer jeans, featuring a cute but ample
behind. Voters probably get the subliminal message that the judicial candidate who has usurped the designer jeans space should be elected because he (or she) is softer, hence more compassionate, than the
opposition. Offended by the election gimmicks used by judges who must
run for office, reform-minded lawyers and professors have urged that all
judges should be appointed. I once submitted my name for an appointed

federal judgeship, and I suggest that the elective process is the better because what you see (even if it is on the back of the 57th Street crosstown) is exactly what you get.

It was during the one-term tenure of President Carter, when there was a window of opportunity for Democrats, that I submitted my name to the Judicial Selection Panel of Senator Daniel P. Moynihan, D-N.Y. I also submitted my resume, a completed confidential official questionnaire, and letters of endorsement from the prominent. As per instructions, 10 copies of everything were provided. I then galvanized all of my energies toward the big moment, my interview with the Sacred Panel.

For about two weeks before that scheduled meeting I studiously reviewed the 10 most important cases of my career, cases that I had listed, chronologically, in response to the panel's request. I reread all of my briefs and all of my opponents' briefs, and analyzed anew each of the judicial opinions. I reasoned that the panel, with its staff of legal experts, would have had several weeks in which to study and analyze each of those litigations, and I prepared myself for questions of the most penetrating sort. And because I had had no experience in the criminal law—I was one of the few candidates who had never been an assistant District Attorney—I purchased a criminal law textbook and studied it with uncommon diligence.

Finally, the day of the interview. I took an extra white shirt to the office, and selected a tie that I had bought at the Metropolitan Museum of Art, a tie with an ancient (second or third century B.C.) North African design. All Metropolitan Museum ties come with a historical note describing the pattern, and I read the one that accompanied the tie that I had chosen; I had the text because the tie was still in its original box, never before having been worn. I read the museum text so that, if during one of the breaks from the intense legal discussion, a panel member would comment on the tie, I would be able to answer that the design was from Carthage, second or third century B.C. I believed, the age of Hannibal.

The interview, held late one afternoon in a panelled conference room of a large downtown law firm, lasted about one minute, or slightly less. Only a few committee members were present, and just as I finished shaking a few hands, I was thanked for appearing and politely dismissed. Since I had not been asked to say one word about anything, I hoped that they had noticed my tie. The thought then occurred to me—since no words other than salutations had been exchanged—that perhaps they chose judges on the basis of their foulards. If so, I had a terrific chance. They could not select judges on the basis of socks, for instance, because they had not seen my socks. And all white shirts were, more or less, alike. And all shoes were shined. The only distinguishing feature, it seemed to me, was one's four-in-hand; and mine, from the Metropolitan Museum of Art, was probably the most beautiful.

When I recounted my experience to a friend more politically astute than I, the explanation was so simple that I was embarrassed at my innocence. Those Senatorial panels, it was explained, were not for picking judges—that was done privately by the Senator and his staff—but for protecting Senators from friends and big contributors. When a large donor advises the Senator, discreetly, that his son or daughter is a successful lawyer and would make a fine judge, the Senator tops the comment by saying that he or she would not be a fine judge, but a great one. However, because the Senator has taken all politics out of judicial selection, the offspring must first be approved by the Merit Selection Panel, manned by distinguished Americans. The donors are assured that as soon as that routine hurdle is cleared, the nomination will be made. Realizing that I had fared no worse than the children of the Senator's largest campaign benefactors—except that my interview was surely shorter, less of a charade—I appreciated how truly democratic the process really was.

But I'm not surprised that I wasn't chosen. I probably lost out to someone wearing a Brooks Brothers rep or a Liberty of London paisley, patterns I could have worn myself had I thought about it more carefully. Or maybe the Judicial Selection Panel favored ties that were solid, indicating a stability that was entirely appropriate for a federal judge, although whether they should be of primary colors or blends was surely a matter that was actively debated. I hope that they tolerated blends, because, frankly, green is among my favorites; but I would assume that orange and purple were never in contention. And there were, I know, fringe candidates who, defiantly, sported polka dots—the "take me because I'm different" type—but they knew that they had no chance, and I agree with the committee's unanimous decision to eliminate them on the first round. Tartans were also favored, because the wearer was proclaiming, in a quiet but forceful way, that like the clans in the highlands, he would honor ancient precedents. But the panel could have concluded that the same pledge could be inferred from solids, but without the haughtiness that a tartan might represent. Geometric patterns were the most difficult to evaluate because often, like optical illusions, they appeared differently from different angles; as a result, a majority of panel members could never completely agree on any such cravat.

I was not chosen, and the fault was mine, entirely. In discussing my candidacy the panel concluded—and I hereby state for the record that I do not disagree—that the number of cases involving Hannibal that come before the federal court in a typical year were too few to warrant my appointment, even if the elephants were included.

January 9, 1991

Rock
of
Ages

In 1927 Babe Ruth hit 60 home runs and batted .356; in his last major league season, 1935, his batting average dropped to .181. Babe Ruth, the Sultan of Swat, had stayed too long. And so had another monarch, King Lear:

> Goneril: You see how full of change his age is . . .
> Regan: 'Tis the infirmity of his age . . .
> (Act I, scene 1)

And so it is that everyone and everything grows old and withers. Everything, that is, except rocks and, perhaps, judges.

Rocks become so old that their age is not measured by the calendar but by radiocarbon dating. Applying a dab of chemical, a scientist might proclaim that this or that particular rock—from the moon for instance—is 10 billion years old, proving to some skeptics that the moon is older than Philadelphia. But although that rock has been around for a long, long time—and this is the point—it is still as hard, as undiminished, as ever.

Like rocks, the life span of judges is infinite, but only by the judges' own steely reckoning. Several states have enacted laws requiring judges to retire at age 70. But the judges, proclaiming their rock-like longevity, have challenged those laws as unconstitutional; they argue that such enforced retirement violates the Equal Protection Clause of the Fourteenth Amendment. One such case, *Gregory v. Ashcroft,* involving Missouri's mandatory retirement of judges at age 70, will soon be heard by the U.S. Supreme Court.

Since everybody else in the world acknowledges that typical 70-year-old people, even those eating oat bran, can no longer run the mile in under four minutes, the narrow question before the High Court is whether judges are more like people or more like rocks.

The judges, of course, claim to be more like rocks. They cite their courageous decisions which, they argue, make them boulder than ordinary folks. And they note, too, that they each gave up pumicing careers at the bar in order to become public servants so that they should not be taken for granite. While the judges consider that these arguments are marbleous, their critics suggest, most deferentially, that that is because they (the judges) drink their own wine by the quartz. But the judges' main point is their independence—they never, they assert, gravel before any special interest, but render every decision fairly and onyxly. In garnetting support for their septuagenarian cause, these judges contacted a wide range of legal scholars, from those who had vigorously opposed the nomination of Robert Bork to those who considered themselves to be bauxites.

But suddenly, before argument, the case ended the way cases often end—by a strange technicality. It seems that the judges' petition, which, jurisdictionally, had to be filed by 5 P.M., was not clocked into the clerk's office until 5:02, too late. The clerk had no choice, and the case was summarily dismissed. When the embarrassed lawyer telephoned and inquired: "How much was the filing tardy by?" the clerk replied, "Bituminous."

What galls these state court judges is that federal judges, no sturdier than they, enjoy (courtesy of the Constitution) lifetime tenure. It is galling because while they (the state court judges) are forced to play golf or read poetry, their federal colleagues are still gaveling away, giving jail sentences to the unrepentent, lecturing whomever chances to be in court, basking in the "Your Honor" salutation, donning those magic robes, still issuing orders and decrees, still going to bar association dinners on the cuff, and still believing that they are immune from the decline of age. There is, of course, a simple solution to this intra-court discrepancy: Federal judges, too, should be retired at age 70, which was far beyond the average life span in 1787, when the Constitution was adopted. George Washington died as an old man, at age 67.

One of the saddest days in my professional life was the only day I appeared before the U.S. Supreme Court. For there was Justice William O. Douglas, mountain climber, sitting limp in a wheelchair, wrapped in a blanket, apparently unable to speak. It was understood by all that he didn't want to retire while a Republican was president, and that he hoped to ride out his illness until the next election. But not until I saw him, with his 100-year-old face, did I realize the withered depth of Justice Douglas' frailty.

King Lear stated—incorrectly I suggest—that a judge's "robes hide all" (Act IV, scene vi). King Lear was wrong, because a judge's robes cannot hide his age anymore than Babe Ruth's uniform could hide his.

December 17, 1990

Constitutional
Clauses
and
Causes

Newspaper editors like the First Amendment (you can write whatever you want and the government can't stop you; you can even oppose the invasion of Panama and print a story about Panamanian civilian casualties, although nobody has yet pushed the Amendment that far). Drug merchants and folks with contraband like the Fourth Amendment (the cops can't, willy-nilly, come a-searching). Politicians and other reticent types like the Fifth Amendment (you don't have to answer questions if you don't want to, and thumb-screws are, more or less, passé). Death row residents like the Eighth Amendment (every now and then some judge awakes and rules that capital punishment is cruel). Political science professors like the separation of powers that is spelled out in Articles I, II and III (they can discuss, and with much learning, John Locke and Montesquieu without having read either). Each of us, for reasons selfish or poetic, has our favorite section of the Constitution.

Federal judges, the subject of this essay, prefer the clause in Article III Section 1 that states that judges shall receive "a Compensation, which shall not be diminished during their Continuance in Office." In 1989

Congress made federal judges part of the national Social Security system, and so, beginning with January 1, 1984, federal judges, like all of the rest of us, had Social Security taxes subtracted from their pay checks.

That deduction, claim the judges, violates their favorite Constitutional clause because, they argue, it diminishes their pay. Although they frequently lecture others about clogging the courts with frivolous lawsuits, a group of federal judges has actually banded together and filed a complaint challenging the constitutionality of their Social Security payments. Their logic is that any government action that reduces their net pay is, *ipso facto*, unconstitutional. If they win—and anything is possible since their case will be heard, of course, by one of their fellows—the judges will then possess the most dangerous of all legal engines, a precedent.

A precedent starts with the innocence of Adam and Eve, but the progeny can be dangerous. If the Social Security argument prevails, the next step would be to nullify, for sitting federal judges only (see Art. III Sec. 1 of the United States Constitution), the recent subway fare increase (for paying $1.15 per ride instead of $1.00 certainly "diminishes" judicial pay). And with the subway precedent, the inevitable next step would be a petition before the Florida Citrus Commission demanding that the price of tangerines (I choose the example of tangerines because I eat four or five or six every day; I love them) be fixed, but only for those special persons covered by Article III Section 1, to the prices prevailing before the recent frost. And as the precedents proliferate to include every known item of expense, a jurisprudential point, hitherto obscure, will begin to clarify.

The argument of Original Intent, advanced by conservative jurists as a seeming philosophical contention to restore constitutional truths to the truth of 1787, turns out to be nothing but the first step in pegging prices that federal judges must pay to the levels that prevailed as of September 17, 1787, the date on which George Washington gaveled the Constitutional Convention to a close. Any higher price, on any commodity, would clearly be unconstitutional.

As for the argument that, by the same reasoning, judges should be paid only the salaries that were in effect back then (rather than the

$96,600 yearly stipend that takes effect on February 1, 1990), the black robed crew laughed and howled and roared until they could laugh and howl and roar no more. The constitution, they pointed out, only prohibits judicial salaries from being diminished; it says nothing about increases.

And so, as they always do, federal judges got their way—except when they tried to explain to their local greengrocer why the United States Constitution entitled them to buy a bushel of tangerines for six cents.

January 12, 1990

The Appalachian Trail Is Beautiful

The nomination of two men with scant judicial records (David Souter and Clarence Thomas) to be Justices of the U.S. Supreme Court has been justified on the ground that the President must choose only persons who have no paper trail. For it was his paper trail, administration spokesmen mourn, that led to the Senate defeat of Robert Bork.

When Oliver Wendell Holmes retired from the Court in January 1932, President Herbert Hoover's keenest advisers convened to choose his successor. Their principal task, they explained, was to avoid a nominee with a paper trail, a nominee who would be Borked. What with the Depression, they explained, the President didn't need the further embarrassment of having his Supreme Court choice rejected by the Senate.

With that single purpose in mind—picking a person who did not have a record that could be challenged either by the voracious liberal media or by the Democratic sharks in Congress—a short list of safe candidates was prepared for the President's final consideration.

Heading the list was Harpo Marx. As one of the President's men explained, the Judiciary Committee could spend weeks, or even months, interrogating him, but he'd still not speak about his position on either abortion or natural law. The only negative—it was a negative because the President was known to prefer modest people—was the fact that Mr. Harpo Marx sometimes tooted his own horn.

The second recommended name, Rudolph Valentino, had a question mark written along side. He was, they said, both strong and silent—two qualities that the President most admired—but (and that was the reason for the question mark) no one knew for certain whether Mr. Valentino actually talked when he was off the screen. If he did, it would not be fatal (according to the White House wise men) because he would be instructed to smile and even to kiss, but not to talk, during the two weeks of his confirmation hearings.

The third name, Oliver North, was somewhat of a surprise. The White House advisers' theory was that even though Mr. North did have strong views on many issues relevant to the confirmation hearings, it would not matter because he could be counted on not to tell the Senators the truth.

But President Hoover ignored his brilliant and politically astute sages and chose, instead, Benjamin Nathan Cardozo. The President's advisers were aghast, for the nominee had a paper trail that was longer than the Appalachian Trail; and as it wended its way through the bramble bushes of the law it took more non-Borkian turns than any other path in the legal forest. As a judge (from 1914 to 1932) on New York State's highest court, the Court of Appeals, Cardozo had written hundreds of opinions, many of which did what the President's gurus considered to be sinful— they broke new ground. In *MacPherson v. Buick Motor Company*, for instance, Judge Cardozo ruled that a person who bought a defective Buick automobile—one wheel was made of imperfect wood and its spokes crumbled—could sue the Buick Motor Company. (Before that decision it was the general rule that a purchaser of a defective car could sue only the dealer from whom he had bought it; but that dealer had a complete defense: he was not responsible because it was, obviously, the manufacturer's fault. The dissent argued that Mr. MacPherson should not recover from the Buick Motor Company, but should sue, instead, the Imperial Wheel Company of Flint, the manufacturer of the crumbled wheel.)

But what frightened the President's advisers even more than his ground-breaking decisions were the nominee's judicial writings, particularly as they appeared in two of his books, *The Nature of the Judicial*

Process and *The Growth of the Law.* The advisers had been taught that such ideas had been repealed by the Constitutional Convention of 1789 and were no longer mentioned in the presence of ladies:

> I take judge-made law as one of the existing realities of life.
>
> For every tendency, one seems to see a counter-tendency; for every rule its antinomy. Nothing is stable. Nothing absolute. All is fluid and changeable. There is an endless "becoming."
>
> It is true, I think, today in every department of the law that the social value of a rule has become a test of growing power and importance.
>
> From all this, it results that the content of constitutional immunities is not constant, but varies from age to age.

Despite having a paper trail that extended from Canada to the Gulf of Mexico, Benjamin Nathan Cardozo was confirmed by the Senate. Nevertheless, the Administration still argues that having a paper trail is fatal to a Supreme Court nominee. Because of that stubborn adherence to principle, the biggest obstacle facing Clarence Thomas is the rumor that, as a poor boy in Pin Point, Ga., he once had a newspaper route. That would be fatal, some literal presidential aides have privately conceded, because having a paper route is almost the same as having a paper trail.

October 2, 1991

V
Reflections on Recent Wars

Noah's
Ark
1989

The principal cause of the War of 1812, said the teacher (Miss Curtis, who taught history at P.S. 152 in Brooklyn), was that American seamen were impressed by the British. It was the most baffling history lesson we ever had and, even now, almost 50 years later, some of my classmates are still afraid to applaud too hard at a Shakespeare play for fear of starting a war with our most reliable ally.

I thought of the War of 1812 the other day when I read in the *New York Times* that the U.S. Navy had captured dolphins in the Gulf of Mexico and was training them to guard the Trident Nuclear Submarine Base at Bangor, Wash. It seems that the dolphins' sonar, developed over millions of years (and without a dime from the Defense Department), is far superior to man's.

The Navy has justified the kidnappings on the ground of American national security. Various animal groups have filed suit in the Seattle federal court, but the guess is that the dolphins' sonar is better than their legalese, and that in the give-and-take of the courtroom Man will prevail. And that will be too bad, because whereas the War of 1812 involved only an indecisive struggle between two countries separated by an ocean, the combat tactics begun by the Navy this time may engulf our planet.

The Soviets, of course, have not been idle. They promptly captured *their* dolphins and trained them to defend *their* vital undersea interests. And then both sides trained additional dolphins to penetrate the other's defenses, both by force (using the strongest males) and by Mata Hari techniques (using nubile females).

With all the word's dolphins thus deployed on one side or the other (with some shuttling back and forth as spies and counter-spies), the respective navies, eager to achieve the maximum advantage, conscripted the sharks. And soon all of the world's sharks were impressed into service, reporting either to San Diego or to Vladivostok. And then the crocodiles and alligators, to protect the rivers. And then those icky jellyfish, to protect the coastline against invasion.

With every seaborne tooth and tentacle thus geared for battle, the land armies became jealous of the awesome but amazingly inexpensive forces marshaled by the fleets. And so the generals—both in Washington and in Moscow—sent rival recruitment teams into Africa and Asia to bid for the services of lions, tigers and cheetahs. And, in the most impenetrable forests known to man, suddenly there appeared, tacked to trees and suspended from branches, rival posters, in English or Russian, enticing the animals to learn a trade while they served as mercenaries. The lures were great, and only the elephants refused to be stampeded. Dancing bears from the Russian circus sent letters—the United States has charged that they were coerced—to their kinsmen at the Arctic Circle extolling the virtues of glasnost and the joys of pirouetting through Gorky Park.

The air forces—ours and theirs—became embarrassed by the huge costs of spy satellites and Stealth bombers, and so special sign-up bonuses were offered to all qualifying hawks and eagles. No formal education was needed, but one had to pass a rigid eye examination. Sparrows and bluebirds were organized to watch and report, much like the air-raid wardens of World War II, although it was very hard to know, as you spotted, whether a given bird was ours or theirs.

Having marshaled all the animals and trained them for combat, each side was poised and ready. The next war would *really* be a world war not, as in the past, just some battles among humans. The strategists and think-tank thinkers, on both sides, began to ponder the frightful consequences should a war be launched, for this time everything might be destroyed. Everything, that is, except the cockroaches. Scientific studies confirmed that even if there were a nuclear holocaust, most cockroaches would survive. The question then would be, would they be *our* cockroaches or *their* cockroaches? So, in every old tenement in New York and Moscow—and in Chicago and Leningrad—there appeared, instead of the old lethal sprays and Flit-guns, announcements promising a medical school scholarship for any qualified roach who served his (or her) country with a four-year hitch. It was a very effective campaign because medical school was, for the average inner-city roach, prohibitively expensive.

May 11, 1989

Red Cloud
Listens
to the
Great
Debate

I t snowed in New York on Friday afternoon, January 11,
1991, the Friday before the Armageddon Day of January
15. So rather than return downtown to my office in the
Woolworth Building I decided to go directly to my daughter Amy's doctor's office, where I was to meet her and take her out for a light supper.
Since I would have plenty of time I decided to walk from Third Avenue
and 47th Street to Park and 90th, and even then I would be early, although walking in the snow was slower going. I decided to buy a book
in the first bookstore that I passed so that I'd have something to read
while Amy was being examined. I chanced by the Canterbury Book Shop
on Lexington, between 74th and 75th Streets, and went in both to
browse (using up some time) and to make a selection. After thumbing
through a few poetry collections, I purchased Dee Brown's *Bury My
Heart at Wounded Knee.* I started it while waiting in the doctor's office,
and read most of it at home on Friday night between the War Powers
orations carried live by PBS from the floor of the U.S. Senate Chamber.

I finished the book on Saturday morning, just about the time the oration ended and the vote began.

As the book begins, President Andrew Jackson, called Sharp Knife by the Indians because he had led his troops in the slaying of thousands of Cherokees, Chickasaws, Choctaws, Creeks and Seminoles, proposed separating whites and Indians by giving the Indians most of the lands west of the Mississippi River. And, in keeping with that principle, the Congress (on June 20, 1834) passed a law (*An Act to Regulate Trade and Intercourse with the Indian Tribes and to Preserve Peace on the Frontiers*) dedicating all territory west of the Great River to the Indians, except for the states of Missouri and Louisiana and the Territory of Arkansas. The rest of the book details how the whites violated that law by overrunning every square inch of land right up to the Pacific Ocean. In the process, the Indians were slaughtered, lied to, cheated, raped, tortured, impoverished, humiliated and destroyed, all because the whites had military superiority. And gone forever are the Sioux, Dakotas, Utes, Navahos, Nez Perces, Poncas, Iroquois, Apaches, Seminoles, Pueblos, Cheyennes, Osages, Omahas and a dozen other tribes of brave people who loved their ancestral land. The making of one indivisible nation between the two great oceans was, declaimed the whites, their Manifest Destiny.

After the assassination of Sitting Bull (in December 1890), Red Cloud was the last of the great Sioux Chiefs, the last of the great Indian Chiefs. Red Cloud, made vividly alive by Dee Brown's account, spoke: "There was no hope on earth, and God seemed to have forgotten us." His words were so relevant to the day's unfolding events that I invited him to join me as I watched the Great Debate from the Senate Chamber. Red Cloud soon became riveted to the TV set as speaker after speaker seemed to apologize for the way in which the Indians had been treated.

"We cannot permit conquest by force," intoned Senator after Senator, and tears of joy came to Red Cloud as he envisioned the return of the Sioux and the buffalo to the Great Plains, the return of the Mohawk to their hunting ground where the river always flowed. "All the conquered land must be returned," intoned Senator after Senator, and how Red Cloud wished that Geronimo, Big Eagle, Little Crow and Crazy Horse could have lived to share this day, the day when the white man finally understood that conquest by force was wrong. "It is never too late for justice," said Red Cloud, "as long as the sun rises and sets."

But Red Cloud noticed, as he listened more intently, that the only tribe being mentioned for rescue was the Kuwaitis. He told me that he had hunted with the Kowtoliks and had fished with the Klamaths, but had never before heard of the Kuwaitis, the tribe whose conquest seemed to have so aroused the consciences of the Great Council in Washington. And so I explained that the Kuwaitis lived not in the mountains of the Great Rockies where the sun kissed the snow every day whether summer or winter, but in a place far distant, called the Persian Gulf, and that their conquerors were not members of the U.S. Army Cavalry, but were Iraquis, a tribe of fierce fighters whose chief, one Saddam Hussein, was hated for his violent ways. I explained that it was to free the Kuwaitis from the Iraquis that the Senators had voted to go to war, and that no one in the Senate had suggested that the same standard be applied to the lands west of the Mississippi, lands that had been sacredly pledged to the Indians by President Andrew Jackson over a century and half ago.

While all the Senators were busily congratulating themselves, intoning to each other that their speeches had been unique contributions to political discourse, Red Cloud yawned and turned off the TV. "My people," he said, "communicated by smoke signals. The messages got through almost as fast as they do on your television because we did not allow commercials. Whole treaties were sent, in elegant plumes, across the Great Plains in no time at all, if time be gauged by the evergreen tree. But even if the entire *Encyclopaedia Britannica* had been translated into Sioux, and then transmitted from Oregon to Florida, there would have been less puffery than I just heard from your Senate floor."

January 25, 1991

The Penny
Arcade

Coney Island was only a half-hour train ride away, and I spent many Sunday afternoons of my childhood enjoying its fading, but still gaudy, splendors. When I was very little, six or seven and maybe even eight, I'd go there with my father; we'd climb the many steps to the Avenue J station at East 16th Street (Brooklyn), and board the southbound Brighton Local to the last stop. I would stand in the first car, looking out the front window at the tracks and signals ahead; my father would always bring a paper to read. We never spoke much, on the train or elsewhere. My favorite Coney Island ride was the carousel; I'd always mount a white horse that went up and down; the motionless horses, those that went around and around but never up and down, were, I thought, for girls. As I got a little older, a more toughened young man of eight, I also tried the bumper cars; the object of the bumper car, which was electric powered (a metal rod, attached to the back of the car, brushed against a steel meshing that was suspended a few yards above, producing the power), was to crash into another car, broadside if possible, so as to turn the victim's car around. The cars were surrounded by wide rubber bumpers so that no damage was done by the jolts to either man or machine. When my father took me "bumping" he would watch from the sideline while I drove recklessly about. But at about the age of eight or nine I began to go to Coney with my friends, and then the great sport was to bump each other. I never went on the carousel when only with my friends because I thought that that might be considered effete. And when we began to outgrow the bumper car we moved, hesitantly, to the Cyclone, the most daredevil of Coney's roller-coasters. A true sign of manhood was riding in the front car. I did it often, and hated it every time.

One of the last times I went to Coney Island with my father is the time I remember most vividly. It was Sunday, September 1, 1939, and as we headed for home we entered the cavernous subway station at Stillwell Avenue—it was the terminal not only for the Brighton Line, but for the Sea Beach and West End lines as well—a newspaper vendor hawked "War Declared—Read All About It." The headline on the tabloid said, in large block type, just one word: "War." Germany had invaded Poland, and England and France had responded by declaring war. I was confused by the ambiguity, because war I knew was always bad, but finally facing up to Germany I knew was considered to be good. I knew that war was always bad because Mom was always singing "I didn't raise my boy to be a soldier, I raised him up to be my pride and joy." The verse ended with lines about not killing some other mother's darling son. As the war clouds darkened, Mom, I guess, just thought of my older brother and me, and wondered if we'd be war's casualties, as had been one of her brothers in World War I.

War's effect on Coney Island, since the United States was neutral until Pearl Harbor, could be seen only in the penny arcade. One penny, dropped in a slot, gave you 30 exciting seconds to shoot at German warplanes. After the penny dropped, your machine gun was activated; a light in the cylinder went on and as you peered through a glass lens at your end of the tube you could see a revolving disk, with painted Messerschmitts flying in formation at the far end, about a yard away. The object was to get a Messerschmitt in your gun's cross hairs, and then pull the trigger. The gun vibrated a little when activated, and the war was simulated rather well considering it was all for one penny. Even though no enemy craft may ever have fallen from the painted revolving disk, nonetheless I shot down thousands of them before peace came in 1945. I realized it only later, but all the planes we shot at in those early days were German, never Italian; Japanese Zeros were not painted on the little revolving screens until December 7, 1941. It all reflected Brooklyn's population, largely Jewish and Italian. Even today I can't recall the names of any Italian warplanes, for they were never the enemy at Coney Island, even after Italy invaded France and President Roosevelt had spoken about the hand that held the dagger.

The most wonderful thing about the penny arcade war was that the enemy never fired back; not once during the entire conflict was I in any danger. But I probably lost some of my gung-ho enthusiasm as the war went on and as I grew up. In 1939 I was very short, and could only use those penny war games that had a box on the floor under the slot, or else I was not able to reach the eye level of the tube, not even if I stood on my tiptoes. But as the war dragged on, I grew and matured; and by war's end I was not only easily tall enough, but also understood what the real war and the real Holocaust meant. If only, I thought, the real war could be fought by shooting make-believe bullets at make-believe airplanes flying in painted formation in a make-believe sky.

I had not thought about that penny arcade war for years and years. But it all came back when CNN began to show, every night, pictures, cleared by U.S. censors, of bombing scenes in the Persian Gulf war. The enemy target was always centered in one of our rocket's cross hairs. A few seconds into the picture and we see an explosion, precisely at the spot where the cross hairs pinpoint. And in all those pictures, the enemy has never fired back, not even once.

If I close my eyes and let my mind wander back in time, the CNN pictures and my penny arcade memories begin to merge; the bad guys, always caught in cross hairs, are destroyed by a sudden burst of gunfire. Games and war, childhood and now, become vaguely interchangeable. One can almost see our leaders and military officers (especially those who give those illustrated briefings from headquarters in Saudi Arabia) playing at the penny arcade, peering through the glass lens of a cylinder, then pulling the trigger. It would be better if they had chosen, instead, to ride the carousel. Then they could mount white horses that go 'round and 'round to Calliope's breathless but patriotic rhythms, prancing proudly but causing no deaths.

February 21, 1991

VI
Law Schools and
Law Firms
(Both Stodgy)

Attaché
Cases and
Gunnysacks

A law firm in Chicago, McKenzie & Baker, has proudly announced a landmark event—the aggregate number of lawyers in its forty-two offices worldwide has reached 1,000. But 1,000 attaché-toting lawyers, signing documents in wood-panelled conference rooms located on the upper floors of glass-towered office buildings in such places as New York, London, Paris, Rome, Rio de Janeiro and Hong Kong is not the millennium.

Leading law firms have not always been quite so elegant or quite so large. In the 1840s and 1850s, the most prominent law firm in Illinois was not the McKenzie & Baker horde from Chicago, but Lincoln & Herndon, a two-man operation based in Springfield.* While young Billy tended the home office, Mr. Lincoln covered all 15 counties of the state's Eighth Judicial District and the more populous counties of the Seventh, concentrating on Logan, Tazewell, Menard and Woodford. He covered that vast territory (estimated to be 120 miles long and 160 miles wide, at its widest) by horseback and by buggy. He would sleep in farmhouse bedrooms furnished only with a bed, a wash basin and a spittoon; sometimes he would sleep in a tavern's common room with a dozen other

*The facts concerning Lincoln & Herndon are taken from Carl Sandburg's *Abraham Lincoln*.

lawyers. And sometimes, to keep a court date, he would ride through the night, despite the winter cold or the spring thaw, keeping his papers and notes in a burlap gunnysack.

Modern big law firms have a modest dilemma: They want, of course, to be rich and powerful and grand, but they would like, without sacrificing any of their grandeur, to be *perceived* as humble and fair, to be *perceived* as having a touch of Abraham Lincoln. And so almost all of the mighty firms, as a token of their humility, hang, somewhere in their vast offices, at least one picture of Mr. Lincoln. Since the picture is symbolic only, it never hangs in the main reception area alongside one of those grim eponymous partners. Nor does it hang in the firm's main library, because if there it might inspire young lawyers to do something other than corporate mergers. Mr. Lincoln's picture hangs, rather, on some obscure wall, usually between the xerox room and the messenger lounge, a framed reminder to all who pass that greatness can come from a humble start.

I have, in my own one-man office, two pictures of Mr. Lincoln. One is a colored picture postcard, from the John Hay Library at Brown University, that I keep under my desk's glass top. The other is a full-length lithograph that hangs on the wall in front of me as I work, next to a picture of George Washington. My Lincoln picture depicts the President in formal dress, with his left hand resting on a table on which sits a quill pen in an ink bottle, a pile of state papers (including ones entitled "Constitution," "Union," and "Proclamation of Freedom"), and several bound volumes (including two entitled *Jefferson's Works*). Resting on the floor, just to Mr. Lincoln's right, is a globe and an American flag.

While window shopping in the bric-a-brac stores that line MacDonald Avenue (in Brooklyn), Mom spotted the Lincoln portrait sitting among several broken wicker chairs and an old coatrack with missing hooks. I had just begun my one-man practice, and Mom said that she could not imagine a more wonderful present. "Mom," I said, "I'm no Abraham Lincoln, so I think that it may be a bit pretentious." She replied: "Mordecai, since you have to have *some* lawyer's portrait on the wall, why not use a man with a Biblical name?" Not able to overcome that logic, I reluctantly agreed, and that picture (together with the one of George Washington) has been on my wall ever since. When lawyers from those large firms visit, I tell them that the portraits are of my firm's founding partners. But no one has ever smiled when I said that; lawyers from those large firms rarely smile, unless a judge makes a poor joke.

Although they all have his picture on the wall somewhere, Abe Lincoln, the lawyer, was never able to obtain a job offer from any of them. "Mr. Lincoln," they told him, "your resumé is very interesting. We've never had an applicant before who was President of the United States. But our offices are in places like New York, Paris, London and Rome, and we don't think you'd be comfortable here with your Gettysburg address."

January 5, 1988
(revised for this book)

An Anniversary
of Sorts

In the end, the firm failed because the stationer could not find a solution. It had been the first law firm in the world to have (simultaneously) 1,000 partners. When that historic plateau was reached, it was celebrated by black-tie dinners in each of the firm's 39 offices worldwide. The firm was the envy of the profession not only because of its record number of partners, but because it was designed with a perfect internal balance that was impervious to economic pressures. It had a large mergers and acquisitions division whose function was to coin money in boom times, and an equally large bankruptcy group whose function was to fund the firm's expenses and the partners' needs when the cycle spiraled lower.

The geographic calibration was also perfect: there was an office in New York and an office in Rio de Janeiro, so whether a client needed winter or needed summer, the firm was ready. There was even a fully staffed office in Moscow, just in case a smoldering White counterrevolution should return the Romanovs, finally, to power. The point the firm's PR brochure underscored was that this was the one firm that had considered—and prepared for—every eventuality.

And so it had been since the summer of 1964, when the firm was founded by four acquaintances, each of whom had just been passed over for partner; the four vowed this would never happen to them again. They subleased space in a midtown loft between Sixth and Seventh Avenues

132

in New York City and, in a conference room shared with accountants and furriers, planned their future growth and success. There is no point in detailing each bold step in the journey that led to that first-to-have-1,000-partners record, but suffice it to say that it was considered to be the law-firm equivalent of the 1521 voyage of Ferdinand Magellan.

But then, just as the firm was celebrating its twenty-fifth anniversary, just as it had reached the magic figure of 1,000 partners, the stationer failed. It was the one glitch that no one had foreseen, especially since the in-house stationer was known to be the finest in the world. He had served as the private engraver to the Queen of England; his forebears had been royal engravers and stationers since the Tudors. His background and ge-nius notwithstanding, the problem seemed insoluble.

In a nutshell, how could 1,000 names fit on one letterhead? When printed to leave room on the page for a date, an address, a salutation, a message, and a closing, the names were writ so small that they could be read only by the Pentagon's highest-resolution electronic magnifier. To the naked eye, the top half of the page appeared as a black glob, as if an Exxon oil tanker had discharged its cargo right there. The stationer, being a practical man, suggested, as an obvious alternative, that the firm abandon the traditional 9 × 12 paper and use sheets that measured 36 × 48. At those dimensions, all the names could be read under a simple microscope. Elated to find so simple a solution, the firm ordered a 3-month stationery supply.

But on the very day of delivery, more problems surfaced. There was no typewriter carriage or printer in the office—perhaps in the world—that would accept 36 × 48 paper. Not only could no letter be typed, none could be faxed because there was no fax machine designed for paper so large. Worst of all, no such letter could be mailed because no mailbox slots were big enough. At least the postal problem, the firm thought, could be remedied.

A delegation of senior partners, including former judges, senators, governors, ambassadors, and generals, went to Washington to urge the president to redesign mailboxes to accommodate the larger envelopes. The president was, of course, sympathetic and understanding, since this was already a kinder and a gentler land. But what with Gramm-Rudman constraints and the savings and loan debacle, he doubted that the Congress would appropriate the $5.1 billion needed to change the width of every mailbox slot in America. While Congress debated the issue, more and more letters and bills were fed into the firm's computer, but they had no way of coming out. Finally, the word-processing equipment exploded. And the firm disintegrated.

There were many eulogies, several noting the irony that failure had come of the very stuff of success. But, of course, what is "success" is the ultimate question. In "The Road Not Taken," Robert Frost suggests that success might be in taking (or in liking to think one has taken) the second road.

> I took the one less traveled by,
> And that has made all the difference.

But since the law firm of division strength preferred the first road, the one on which the herd travels, its demise was probably inevitable. For, by the poet's gauge, being one's own man is what makes all the difference.

July 1989

Dean
Polonius

As between the gnomic Polonius and the questioning Hamlet, Professor Robert Clark, dean of the Harvard Law School, chose Polonius. In his welcoming address to the incoming class of '92, the dean advised:

• . . . be true to yourself and your interests.
• Be true to yourself in selecting courses.

And for those students who were a little slower, he added:

• The important thing is for you to be true to yourself.

Other wisdom sprinkled among the dean's remarks include:

• Argue about ideas and interpretations, but avoid competing.
• Eschew anxiety about your career.

I wish that someone had given me that kind of solid advice when I was a law student, because had I known that I was supposed to eschew anxiety I would have been spared a lifetime of worry. It began when Mom asked if I'd be graduating first in my law school class, and (despite the answer) she then asked if I would be offered a clerkship on the United States Supreme Court anyway, and then if I thought that I'd be hired by one of those high-paying fancy law firms that hired graduating lawyers by the carload, and then whether I'd ever be hired by anybody (I went an unusually long time without a job after graduating from law school), and it would have been calming had I been able to tell her that in discussing one's career one of the law's first principles was to "eschew anx-

135

iety." If you say "eschew anxiety" real fast, at the blinding speed at which little girls used to say "'A' my name is Alice, I come from Alabama and my father sells asparagus," all before the ball bounced for the second time—if you could say "eschew anxiety" that fast—a proper response would be "gesundheit." But whether said quickly or slowly, "eschew anxiety" was advice I never received.

The dean's other point, about being true to yourself, is another bit of wisdom I was never given, and certainly not in a setting with 540 other students. But that advice I'm not sorry for having missed, because before one is told to be true to oneself, the preacher should know who his parishioners are. For instance, if some of those incoming freshmen were greedy or mean, being told to be true to themselves would not have been a proper suggestion.

But whether being told to eschew anxiety or to be true to oneself, the problem with the dean's advice is that it dealt only with the surface, only with appearances (did not Polonius tell Laertes that his clothes should be "rich, not gaudy"?). But had Hamlet been his guide, the dean would have spoken to the students about the underlying problems of the law, for the underlying problems of the law, "ay, there's the rub."

The law's most basic question is not whether this or that precedent is correct, but whether (in the spirit of the "to be or not to be" soliloquy) it matters. Imagine going to Harvard Law School for three years, reading thousands of cases and writing hundreds of papers, all the time worrying yourself sick over your class standing (despite the dean's soothing words), only to realize at the end that, except as it affects your income, it all may be irrelevant because the law may be too frail to make a difference. One example of that happened just a few months after the dean's welcoming remarks: In blatant violation of Wyatt Earp's guidelines, a 25,000-man posse, supported by bombers, invaded another country—Panama—killing hundreds and perhaps even a thousand innocent people, all for the purpose of arresting one man who must be presumed innocent, and the whole legal system has been galvanized to try that one presumed-innocent man and all the people who were killed or injured have never been mentioned again because they seem to be irrelevant to the legal process, all of which has made some querulous people suggest that it is the law that may be irrelevant.

The idea that the law, the majestic law, is never more than a muted reflection of the reigning power is, of course, not a new one. It is, rather, an idea borrowed from history and repeated every day. Didn't Achilles kill more people than Dutch Schultz, and always get away with it? I mention Dutch Schultz because I'm in the middle of *Billy Bathgate*. (Mr. Schultz speaks: "The law is not majestic. The law is what public opinion says it is. I could tell you a lot about the law. . . . We got a man to argue for me tomorrow who wouldn't have me to dinner in his house. He talks on the phone with the president. But I have paid his price and he will be at my side for as long as it takes.") And wasn't it Napoleon who said that God was on the side of the heavy artillery? If he didn't say that, he did say, I think, that the Vatican has no divisions. So the suggestion that the law may be irrelevant because it rarely stands against the tide is nothing new, but is simply an idea borrowed from everyday history. To which the dean's response would be: "Neither a borrower nor a lender be."

March 30, 1990

Full Service
Law Firm
of the
Future

In 1921 Karel Čapek, the Czech playwright, accurately described the most advanced American law firms of the 1990s. Mr. Fabry, the chief engineer of *R.U.R.: Rossum's Universal Robots,* speaks:

> One Robot can replace two and a half workmen. The human machine was terribly imperfect. It had to be replaced sooner or later.

Those words demonstrate the essence of progress: machines replace men (or animals). The latest General Electric railroad engine, for instance, replaces 3,800 horses; and the most powerful helicopter engine replaces 6,000 Pegasuses. One farmer today can produce more oat bran than could 165 farmers—or is it 561 farmers?—of his great-grandfather's day.

Only the modern American law firms have defied the logic of the Technology Revolution. Although many law firms are state-of-the-art (one lawyer with a computer terminal can do the legal research in one hour that as recently as 1975 took five and a half days), the firms with the most advanced technology have, perversely, also added the most lawyers.

138

The reason is that the most up-to-date law firms, like gas stations in fancy neighborhoods, want to be "full service" outfits. Such firms routinely describe competitors who have 600 or 700 lawyers as "boutiques," or, to drive home the point, as "mere boutiques."

A genuine, functional full service law firm (FSLF, for short) is necessarily large because it offers advice on any legal issue sought by any client at any time. And so, as the old barriers crumble, and Asian, African, and Eastern European nations join the world's commerce, the FSLF must expand its expertise, *pari passu*.

Each FSLF, to be worthy of its official FSLF designation, is required to have one senior partner, two junior partners, four associates, and eight paralegals qualified to give advice on each of the following legal areas:

The Beirut Building Code, as amended. All structures must be built to be able to withstand mortar shells, bombs, and Western indifference.

The Panama City Parking Regs. Any tank staying for two months must put $1 billion in the meter.

The Beijing Revenue Code. Capital gains rates are lower than capital punishment rates.

The Municipal Edicts of Baku, Birmingham, and Boston, and of all other cities beginning with "B."

Lex non scripta. This is the unwritten law of the United States for high-paying corporate clients because the written laws are often much too fuzzy to be understood.

Dushanbe's Criminal Statutes. Something on which the boutique-sized firms could offer no guidance.

The Laws of Supply and Demand. It's capitalism's creed, but no one has any idea how it works.

Lex Loci. The law of the place, for everyplace, which is the reason that *Lex Loci* is always the largest department of the full service law firm.

Lex Talionis, the law of sweet revenge that will keep the Earth spinning long after the other planets in our solar system have disappeared; for that reason FSLFs will be able to keep on billing long after Armageddon.

The Law of Gravity, of special relevance because density is one of the points of this essay.

For each of these narrow corners of the law, the FSLF maintains a fully staffed department. As more and more—and more—lawyers are hired, space (at $55 per square foot), not legal concepts, becomes the challenge. No more partners' corner offices with six windows, soon it's two windows at most; and then one; and then one pane, shared with a colleague; and, finally but inevitably, no window at all.

The lack of light and air is hardly noticed, for each lawyer's focus has become so narrow that neither light nor air is needed. The computers are so costly that they whir all night, and even the most senior lawyers work in shifts. Furthermore, when it is midnight in New York, the FSLF capital, it is noon in the office of at least one of the firm's major clients. Lawyers' cheeks once so rosy (remember those June outings, long ago, and "bring the kids") turn sallow, then metallic. And lawyers who once bounded up the courthouse steps begin to shuffle in place, robot-like, because there is no space for even a mincing step (forward or backward).

As they vaguely remember the old days of light and air, the old days of discussion and debate, a few of the senior partners balk. Radius (a Robot played by John Rutherford in the New York Theatre Guild Production of *R.U.R.: Rossum's Universal Robots*) addresses them, as the curtain falls:

> You will work! You will build for us! You will serve us! Robots of the world, the power of man has fallen. A new world has arisen, the Rule of the Robots, march.

Although the play has ended, the Full Service Law Firm of the Future has just begun. Does anyone want to know the fine in Windhoek, Namibia, for an overdue library book?

July 1990

VII
Some
Literary
Analogies

Trimmin' the Law

When Whitey, the barber in Ring Lardner's *Haircut*, finished readin' the court decisions in *Benjamin v. Coughlin*, he passed them along to Hod Meyers and Jim Kendall, and then how everybody laughed. "Those judges sure write pretty fancy," said Hod, "but they didn't have all the facts just quite right."

The facts, by then, were well known, sort of. It seems that there was a religious group called the Rastafarians which believed it was a sin to have your hair cut, and so their locks grew and grew. Now that may sound strange, but it really ain't. There are all kinds of religious beliefs out there as to what is sinful. Some folks don't eat pork, some don't use condoms, some don't use guns, some don't cuss. So not havin' your hair cut seems pretty normal. But the New York State Department of Correctional Services ("DOCS" they call it) had a rule that all prison inmates had to have their pictures taken with short hair. So that's how it became what you call a federal case. Of course the solution was simpler than still-made hooch: If the prison officials wanted a picture of these fellas' faces all they had to do was to tie their hair in the back with a rubber band, the way grandma used to do. When the courts were told about how easy it was to take their pictures and still not cut their hair, all the judges held that the government directive was unconstitutional. But for reasons nobody understands—of course none of the boys pretends to be a lawyer—the DOCS folks argued their case all the way up to the U.S. Supreme Court in Washington. But what with all the other things those judges have to do they just refused to listen. So the opinions as written in the lower courts now stand: they can't cut these fellas' hair. I told them that if they couldn't find a rubber band, grandma would lend them hers. But although I've read those opinions over and over, none of them got the facts just exactly right. So let me supplement the official court records to let you know *exactly* what did happen.

When this fella with the very long hair came in—I'd never seen him before, but that didn't surprise me none because we get a lot of travelin' salesmen types who want to look neat to impress the customers—I asked him how he wanted his hair cut. And he says, quick as a trigger, that he didn't want it cut in any style. Well Hod Meyers, who was quite a card, says to him, "Where do you go when you don't want milk, to Fred's Dairy?" That really busted 'em up, but this fella with the long hair didn't laugh none. In fact, he was sort of morose, which was noticeable because that was a Saturday morning when everyone else was bouncy. He just said, sort of flat, "Mr. Barber, don't cut one hair." Well it ain't often that I have a customer who comes in and waits his turn just to tell me not to cut his hair, so I was taken aback. But then I noticed that his friend was wearing a badge, a regular law officer badge with a number and everything. At first I thought that maybe it was a joke, because even our local sheriff doesn't go around sportin' a badge. But one look at that fella and you knew he was a real serious lawman. His voice was more serious still. "Give 'em a haircut, and cut it short," he orders. So I says—and this made Jim Kendall break up—I says, "You don't look like his mother to me." But while everyone else was laughin', this fella with the badge and this fella with the hair are grim lookin'. Then the officer pulls out a paper from his pocket—a paper with a seal that says "State of New York"— and says that it was an official order requiring this long-haired fella to have his hair cut. I ain't never heard before that the government can make a man cut off his hair, but suddenly I'm thinking that that's probably the most intelligent government order since the Declaration of Independence. I started to think of all the folks with long hair who'd have to come to me in order to comply with the Government's new regulation, that is, they'd have to come to me unless they wanted to go all the way up to Carterville. I was thinkin' that after payin' taxes all my life the government finally did somethin' useful. I figured I'd have to hire three, maybe four, assistants, except I'd call 'em apprentices so that they couldn't go out and open their own shops. So I asked this fat fella with the badge if he wanted me to give him a list of the names of other fellas with long hair so he could round 'em up and bring 'em to my shop—I said Tuesday morning was the least crowded—but he says it's only for prisoners in jail. So Hod pops up and says that you wouldn't think that those fellas was able to do that much courtin', and that brought the house down. Everyone laughed, that is everyone 'cept the fella with the long hair and the heavyset fella with the badge. The fella with the long hair just said again what he'd said before: "Mr. Barber, don't cut one hair." The official fella then says to the fella with the long hair, "None of your back-talk," and hands me this official paper that orders me to cut this other fella's long hair. "And it ain't so he can go courtin' neither," he says, "it's so that we can take a good picture of him so if he tries to escape folks will know what he looks like." And with that, the fella with the badge says, "The law is the law, and I'm not in the mood for some kind of debate. I'm takin' a walk around the block, may even grab me a ham sandwich, and when I gets back I expect that the law will have been carried out." And out he stomps like he was the county marshal, except that our marshal ain't never lost his temper. So here I am with this official order over my head, and this guy whose hair it is who says his religion don't let him or anybody else cut it. So I'm in a fix. Just then the preacher comes in. He usually does on Saturdays to look real neat for his Sunday sermon. Now the preacher ain't one to violate any man's religious belief and when I tell him my fix he says that Jesus had long hair and probably so did Moses. But if it's a picture they need, why don't we just tie this fella's long hair up neatly in a bun in the back of his head. I asked the fella if the preacher's ideas would be OK and he said, thankful like, sure as long as you don't cut it. So that's what I did, and to make it look even better, I tied it up real neat and then put some talcum around his ears and on the back of his head as I would have had I used the scissors. Just then the badge fella comes back, looks at this prisoner, and says, "That's fine, we'll take a real clear picture now so if he tries to escape we'll be able to track 'im down." So I says that I ain't a barber who does work on credit, especially with strangers, and he says of course not, and hands me six bits, which amounted to the biggest tip I'd gotten that month.

About a second after they left, maybe less, Jim says how could such a silly dispute go all the way up to the U.S. Supreme Court in Washington and that being a lawyer must be a whole lot less important than being a barber. And Hod said that while it was that long-haired Rastafarian fella who sat in my swivel chair it was the State of New York that got clipped. And everybody laughed, even the sour-faced preacher.

November 15, 1990

A Soliloquy

Although both Hamlet and Vito Bianco (an alias) tricked murderers into confessing, Hamlet is the more famous by far, and deservedly so. For whereas Hamlet achieved his goal with style, Vito Bianco (an alias) was, as we shall see, just a lucky plodder.

The royal tableau for Claudius's unwitting admission opened with a flourish of trumpets and kettledrums, followed by trills from a hautboy. And then began the presentation by a wandering troupe of the one-act drama, "The Mousetrap," as amended by Hamlet himself. And before the-play-within-a-play had ended, the new king, by his own spontaneous guilt-ridden response, was ensnared. "Hamlet," Act III, scene ii, is one of the most memorable scenes in literature, for it not only caught a king, but explored and exposed his character.

Vito Bianco's (an alias) technique for trapping his prey, one Lloyd Perkins, was less elegant. But before that drama unfolds (in a prison cell in Montgomery County, Ill., not in the castle at Elsinore, Denmark), these are the background facts, as recited by the U.S. Supreme Court in *Perkins v. Illinois.* The authorities had learned that one Lloyd Perkins was probably the man who had killed one Stephenson (in East Saint Louis, Ill.), but they had no hard evidence. Learning that Perkins was then in a local jail (for an unrelated crime), the police dispatched an undercover agent to pose as a fellow inmate and to befriend the lonely Perkins. When Perkins's confidence had been won, the prison-garbed mole was trained to ask clever questions leading (it was hoped) to Perkins's confession.

147

And that is, more or less, how it actually happened. The legal question before the Supreme Court was whether the confession had been obtained in violation of the rule established in *Miranda v. Arizona,* which requires the police to advise defendants of their rights before they are interrogated. The Court held that *Miranda* did not apply because Perkins, not even aware that he was being questioned, could not have been intimidated into speaking falsely.

Unfortunately, the Court's opinion makes no reference to the colloquy that produced the confession. However, perhaps through proceedings under the Freedom of Information Act or perhaps through more imaginative sources (we are not at liberty to say which), we have obtained a copy of the transcript of the secretly recorded tape that undid Perkins. The microphone, we can report, was hidden in the hollow heel of the agent's left shoe. The agent's assumed name was "Vito Bianco."

Agent: Good morning, Lloyd, my old pal. Boy, I could sure use some more sleep.

Perkins: 'Morning, Vito.

Agent: I'm still sleepy, but I'm starved. Let's go to breakfast.

Perkins: I want to finish my book first.

Agent: You're always reading. TV's enough for me.

Perkins: TV's too violent. The news is all about death and the shows are all about death.

Agent: I guess death is the way of the world. So TV tells it like it is.

Perkins: But the world doesn't have to be that way.

Agent: Listen, Lloyd, it's been that way for a million years—some guy told me it was a billion years—so it ain't goin' to change now.

Perkins: Maybe so. But all the forces of society seem to be tugging the wrong way. Governments kill people by the millions and call it patriotism. Society kills millions by indifference and calls it capitalism. Everywhere you look, people are killing people legally. Just last week I was reading about this drought in Africa. One group was stopping trucks bringing food to another group. These trucks had just traveled hundreds of miles over the bumpiest roads. They even had to wait at one place three days until some flood subsided. But they waited and waited, and then just as they are about to reach their goal, all these starving . . . hey

Vito, are you falling asleep? Can't you keep your eyes open a few more minutes, I'm talking to you.

Agent: Sure Lloyd, sure. It's real interesting what you're saying.

Perkins: So all these trucks are lined up with food, but first they have to cross a river and then they have to go over a mountain, and when it gets dark at night they are afraid that the smell of the food will attract the animals, because the animals, you know, have very keen smell. But they don't want to hurt any animals, because the animals have lived there a long . . . Hey Vito, you're nodding off again. In fact I can hear you snoring. Listen, Vito, I wish you had stayed awake because you're my best buddy and I gotta get a few things off my chest. Vito, if I can't tell you who can I tell? The dumb things I've done in my life. I quit school almost before I could read. Vito, raise your right hand if you're listenin'. Dead to the world as if it were midnight. Maybe you'll hear me in your dreams. Of course not every dumb thing I've done turned out wrong. I once filched a book from a candy store rack because the cover had a picture of this young lady in a very low-cut dress and two big ones, and it turned out to be *Romeo and Juliet*. So I read it anyway because I hate to run a risk of getting caught for nothing. I read the explanations and the definitions at the bottom of the page, and pretty soon I began to get the flow of it. And after that I began to read better and better books, as if, Vito, you would know anything about that. I always supported myself with odd jobs and a little stealing. When this social worker guy once asked me why I wasn't watching more TV—I was doing a month in the county jail for breaking-and-entering—I told him because I preferred to read. He thought that I was being a wise-guy and told me that if I wasn't going to be more cooperative he couldn't help me. I thought then how much I missed those lady social workers, because they were a lot softer. But I guess with all the ladies taking over as lawyers the men have to do something. I've sure done plenty wrong in my time. A lot of petty stealing. I always felt good when I got back home and read a book, a real book Vito, not one of those trashy things the cops read at the police station. Do you know who I got to like the best? Ernest Hemingway, Vito, you'd like Ernest Hemingway. The best thing you'd like about him is you can't fall asleep while you're reading one of his stories. I'll bet if you fell asleep in the middle of one of Ernest Hemingway's stories he'd come right out of the book somehow and poke you one. But of course sometimes stealing even small things can get you into big trouble. I once was going through this beautiful house because the people were on vacation and the cop on the beat told me about it—I gave him $50—when biffo, right in the middle of my examination of the place the people, or some people anyway, returned. I jumped out a window and kept running until I couldn't hear their screamin' after me anymore. That was a lucky escape. I've also had some unlucky escapes. I never carried a gun because if they catch you with a gun it's 10 years minimum. I don't even own a gun. Never owned a gun. Vito, do you own a gun? I guess I should ask if you're dreaming about guns. Of course, you can get into a mess even without a gun if your luck runs out. And boy did my luck run out a few months ago. I've been shaking ever since. I thought at first of confessing to some priest even though I'm not a Catholic, because hearing confessions is their business. I know some guys who have confessed the most awful crimes to priests, and then felt better. That's why they can't have women priests. Some of the things they'd have to hear. . . . But I never told anybody what I did, until now. I guess if you were awake I'd be too ashamed to tell you, because I wouldn't want to lose you as my best friend. Anyway, I was robbing a house in East Saint Louis—there aren't any fancy houses there, only modest ones. But the modest ones don't have all those security systems, and all I wanted was a few bucks. And outa nowhere, without a sound, this big guy appears. So I threw what I was stealing—a candle stick—at him and ran down the stairs and out of the house. The next day I read in the newspaper that I had killed him. Funny, I practically never read the papers because they're too filled with all that violence. Maybe, in my subconscious I was looking for news of what I had done. But I never thought I had killed him. If I hadn't read the papers I'd never have known it myself. What makes me so mad at myself is that I'm more concerned with the freakish way that I learned of it than what I did. If I hadn't read that paper—and why I read it I'll never know—I avoid the papers because all they print is about violence—I'd be a happy man today, getting ready to leave this jail on Monday. But I just can't get that murder out of my mind. Vito, that's why I can't sleep as well as you do. I'll be checking out of this hotel on Monday, but I'm afraid that I'll never be able to escape from myself. Vito, wake up. Wake up. We can still catch some breakfast if we hurry.

July 19, 1990

Abby Brewster, Charles William Davis

C apital punishment won't be truly constitutional until Abby Brewster of Brooklyn, New York—and all the Abby Brewsters in America—are sent to the gallows. Since that will never happen (for which I'm grateful) it means, if the logic of this paragraph is correct, that capital punishment will never be legal. Unfortunately the courts have reached the opposite conclusion.

Although a Miss Elaine Harper, a neighbor of the Brewster sisters (the spinsters Abby and Martha), praised them for their "kindness, generosity and human sympathy," the sisters had a darker side: they had murdered 12 elderly men. Each victim had been invited to dinner and was served, together with the entrée, a glass of elderberry wine home-brewed with a dash of arsenic, a pinch of strychnine and a hint—just a hint—of cyanide.

Each guest, long before the dessert, fell into a sleep from which he never awoke; so as not to make a fuss, the sisters buried each in the basement of their Victorian house. But even the most eager district attorneys never brought the Brewsters to trial because they were, like their neighbor Miss Harper and their 12 corpses, only characters in *Arsenic and Old Lace,* Joseph Kesselring's three-act play that opened at the Fulton Theater in New York in August 1941.

But despite its gruesome subject, *Arsenic and Old Lace* (which starred Josephine Hull in the original Broadway production) is a farce. In this essay, the play represents a farce of a more serious kind, the farce that capital punishment can never be constitutional.

Capital punishment was prevalent in the United States from colonial times until 1972, when the Supreme Court, awakening from a two-centuries doze, suddenly noticed (in *Furman v. Georgia*) that the death sentence was being imposed on "whim" (Justice Douglas), was "totally capricious" (Justice Brennan), and was "wanton and freakish" (Justice Stewart). Hence, held the Court, the death sentence violated the Eighth and Fourteenth Amendments of our Constitution.

Despite the poetic outrage of their rhetoric, I suggest that the Justices in *Furman* missed the real problem, which was not capriciousness. The real problem was then, as it is now, that when focusing on capital punishment the law confuses the crime with the criminal, the murder with the murderer. It wasn't that the law was capricious. Quite the contrary. The real constitutional problem was that the law, predictably, never sent a "nice" person (whatever his crime) to his death, but reserved that punishment for the outcasts.

But since the *Furman* decision was verbalized as prohibiting caprice, many states, ever eager to reimpose capital punishment, responded by legislating "standards." Their point was that "standards" were the jurisprudential opposite of caprice. Those "standards" were directed at both the quality of the murder—and the quality of the murderer.

The quality of the murder itself was divided into two crisp categories, those that were "especially heinous, atrocious and cruel"—warranting the death sentence, and those that were more gently done. That is a sort of Environmental Impact Statement approach to murder, and it seems to mean that if a murder was committed with a silencer, so as not to awake the neighbors, the perpetrator should be spared. No one has analyzed, from the dead man's point of view, just what an "uncruel" murder is, although the law, as enacted and interpreted by the living, seems to put a high priority on neatness.

But the focus of this essay is on the other standard, the one calibrated for the quality of the murderers who were also placed into one of two categories: those whose backgrounds and circumstances were "aggravating," which qualified them for the death sentence, and those whose backgrounds and circumstances were "mitigating," which spared them.

With those two standards firmly in place—one for murders and one for murderers—the Supreme Court, nodding off again, upheld the constitutionality of capital punishment (*Gregg v. Georgia,* 1976). The Court's reasoning was that since only bad murders committed by bad murderers qualified for capital punishment, the selection process was no longer "capricious." But since caprice wasn't the problem, the Court's decision, except for the fact that it is controlling, is not relevant.

Legal standards cannot be applied, like some exotic formula facial cream, to make the law's biggest wart—the inherent unfairness of capital punishment—disappear. *David v. Maynard,* for instance, involved the usual post-*Furman* issue: were the circumstances of the murderer aggravating or mitigating?

The facts were these: The defendant, one Charles William Davis, had murdered one person in 1942, and had been sentenced to life in prison. While on parole in 1977 he married. When his wife had a change of heart, she asked two friends to help her pack and leave. Surprised to find those two helpers in his own apartment and unhappy with their mission, Mr. Davis shot them both. After finding him guilty of murder, the jury was reconvened to hear evidence on the sentence. It all boiled down to one issue: Was Mr. Davis an aggravating or a mitigating type of fellow? The only positive evidence offered on Davis' behalf was testimony by an acquaintance that he (Davis) was "a considerate individual." In these days of media-hype superlatives, that was not a ringing endorsement. But was it just enough to put Davis into the mitigating and not the aggravating column? After all the evidence on Davis' character had been introduced, the trial judge charged the jury:

"You should not allow sympathy, sentiment or prejudice to affect you in reaching your decision."

The jury, after deliberating, sentenced Mr. Davis to death. But on appeal, the United States Court of Appeals for the Tenth Circuit (which sits out West, and may remember the frontier days better than I) reversed. The Tenth Circuit's point was that the trial judge had erred when he admonished the jury not to be swayed by "sympathy" because "sympathy" for a killer is one of the very elements of "mitigating circumstances." The case was remanded so that the jury could reconsider Davis's punishment.

With the jury's sympathy as a guide, the charmless Charles William Davis, who shot three people over a 35-year span, is doomed. But Abby Brewster, who poisoned 12 people in less than three hours, will be spared because she is (according to Mr. Kesselring, who knows her best) "a plump little darling in her late sixties."

December 18, 1989

As Comedy,
'Bonfire'
Is Not
Funny

To quote Nick Bottom, a weaver (*A Midsummer Night's Dream*, Act III, Scene 1): "There are things in this comedy of Pyramus and Thisby that will never please. First Pyramus must draw a sword to kill himself." A more current comedy, Tom Wolfe's *The Bonfire of the Vanities*, suffers from the same disability; it, too, is not very funny.

Superficially, *Bonfire* purports to be an uproarious novel about how the criminal justice system in New York City functions; superficially *Bonfire* is about a very wealthy Park Avenue stockbroker and socialite—the vain and vacant Sherman McCoy—and his fall from grace when his Mercedes hits a black high school honor student late one Tuesday evening on Bruckner Boulevard in the Bronx. All that may be uproarious—especially if your humor runs to Bronx decay—but right in the midst of all the hilarity Mr. Wolfe, like Pyramus, draws his sword for the kill. And that kill is what this essay is about.

Sherman McCoy (the main character, already described), a successful bond trader at the prestigious Wall Street firm of Pierce & Pierce, considers himself to be one of the Masters of the Universe. His now-and-

156

then mistress, the vacuous but luscious Maria Ruskin, is married to the "shadowy" Arthur Ruskin (also described as a "little Jew from Cleveland" who has "hairy paws" and a "ponderous gut"; sometimes, for short, he's just "an old Yid" who is said to be worth more than $100 million). The Assistant D.A. on the McCoy case, one Lawrence Kramer, is forever two-timing his wife Rhoda, but without Lysander's excuse (Puck having applied the magic flower juices on him by mistake); Rhoda, by the way, bears up rather well, although she is described (out of her hearing no doubt) as "a *yenta* in embryo . . . little Gretel from the *shtetl*."

The principal owner of Pierce & Pierce is Eugene Lopwitz, an "outrageous arriviste" who insists that his office furnishings must be authentic English ("library ladders, bow-front consoles, Sheraton legs, Chippendale backs, cigar cutters, tufted club chairs, Wilton-weave carpet"); but despite the provenance of his furniture, Lopwitz's young fourth wife is French (and a countess at that). The judge assigned to the McCoy case is one Myron Kovitsky, whom we first meet as he "propelled a prodigious gob of spit toward the window" of a van holding prisoners who had been yelling vulgar taunts; it was not at all like one of Puck's moonbeams. Judge Kovitsky, for those who are slow, is a "Jewish warrior, a son of the Masada."

Court officer Kaminsky, a minor character, no more important than Peaseblossom, is described as "a real porker," "a tub." Indeed, New York City girth seems to be one of Wolfe's obsessions. Police officer Goldberg has "a big meaty face"; he is also described as "the fat one, with his hideous smile." A rent collector in *Bonfire* is just not your typical waxmustachioed mean man; he is, rather, a "grossly fat" ("well over 250 pounds") Hasidic Jew "bulging out of his liverish skin like a length of bratwurst" (a bratwurst is a pork sausage in case you missed Wolfe's subtlety). The cantor who officiated at a funeral, Cantor Myron Branoskowitz, is "a huge man, a three-hundred pounder" whose high notes were "just this side of yodel" and whose low notes were a "teary cascade of vibrato."

If one had to describe this sample of Wolfe's prose, a quote from Oberon, King of the Fairies (Act III, Scene 2) would be right on the mark: "Flower of this purple dye." By the way, the eulogy at that funeral was given by a United States Senator from New York, Sidney Greenspan, whose "accent was exceptionally vulgar."

The McCoy case was broken wide open by a scurrilous newspaper; its owner, whose "love of yellow journalism was so genuine," is none other than the British magnate, one Sir Gerald Steiner (also known as Dead Mouse). The Steiners lived in a "grotesque flat on Park Avenue" which housed a "ludicrous museum of Bourbon Louis furniture."

There are others, many others. Did I forget Judge Jerome Meldnick, whose "large pale head resembled a Gouda cheese," so described only so that a few pages later he can be said to be "in thick Gouda consternation"?

In life, we each play many roles. In *Midsummer Night's Dream,* Peter Quince, a carpenter, doubles as Prologue in the play within the play; Snug, a joiner, plays Lion; Francis Flute, a bellows mender, plays Thisby; and Nick Bottom, a weaver, plays Pyramus. In *Bonfire,* perhaps Sherman McCoy and Tom Wolfe are one. For isn't that Tom Wolfe we see, albeit in his Sherman McCoy guise, himself the Master of the Universe, rollicking recklessly through New York City in his black Mercedes, knocking a few of us down as he goes?

As *A Midsummer Night's Dream* ends, Puck, alone on the stage, speaks:

If we shadows have offended,
Think but this, and all is mended;
That you have but slumb'red here,
While these visions did appear.

We should apply Puck's advice and treat Wolfe's book as a bad dream to be quickly forgotten. Despite its popularity, at bottom (not a pun; see the beginning of this piece) *Bonfire* is a "weak and idle theme."

March 15, 1989

Mr. Justice Mars Presiding

"**M**ost liberals in the contemporary sense of the word
. . . are uncomfortable with authority, including
military authority, and hate capital punishment."
That purple sentence was not uttered by Vice President-elect Dan
Quayle on the hustings, because it was considered to be too partisan
even for Orange County, California. Its author is rather Judge Richard A.
Posner (of the U.S. Court of Appeals for the Seventh Circuit in Chicago), a man who regularly argues that the problem with the judiciary
is that judges are not neutral.

The quoted language appears in Judge Posner's recent book, *Law and
Literature,* at page 159; it was written in the context of a discussion of
Herman Melville's masterpiece, *Billy Budd, Sailor.* A law school professor
had written that Captain Vere (Captain of the *H.M.S. Bellipotent,* the
man most responsible for the court-martial and hanging of Billy Budd)
was the villain of the book; Judge Posner disagrees, and in the course of
his discussion wrote the sentence quoted above about liberals (on the
one hand) and authority; the military, and capital punishment (on the
other).

I first read *Billy Budd* in high school, because it was the shortest book
on the list. Those who chose *Moby Dick* were considered to be show-offs

159

or teacher's pets or masochists. At that age, at the high school age of literary innocence, it was thought that the purpose of the written word was to convey a story and a moral clearly; suggested hidden or esoteric themes were ridiculed as a distortion (if *that's* what the author meant then he would have so written).

I thought, on that early reading, that both the story and moral of *Billy Budd, Sailor* were perfectly straightforward: Billy, the kindest and gentlest of youths, was impressed into the Royal Navy at the end of the eighteenth century during the never-ending war between England and France. One Claggart, a petty officer on the *Bellipotent*, jealous of Billy's cheerfulness, falsely accuses him of planning an insurrection. When Billy was confronted by his accuser in the presence of Captain Vere (who knew Billy to be a good man and Claggart to be a liar), he was so dumbfounded by Claggart's false accusation that he was unable to speak (Billy had a speech impediment). But his anger was out of control and in frustration he struck Claggart; the blow was, unintentionally, fatal. A drumhead court-martial followed and Billy was convicted of violating the Mutiny Act. He was hanged, and the *H.M.S. Bellipotent* continued on its routine patrol in search of French ships to attack.

The moral to me and to my class of high-schoolers shortly after World War II was clear: In war, even the most innocent are killed; and if the war was one of those pointless ones (i.e., the war between England and France in 1797), the killing was all the more incomprehensible, a slice of the grown-up world that was ridiculous. Neither I nor anyone in the class doubted Billy's innocence, or doubted that Melville's purpose was to show the folly of war. Nor did anyone doubt that had Melville himself been on that court-martial panel he would have voted to acquit.

It was not until recently, some forty years later, that I have become aware of a great debate about whether Billy Budd was, or wasn't, justifiably hanged. The conflict seems to be among lawyers, for it is hard to think that any poet would justify such a grim result. At any rate, the law professor has suggested that the court-martial was improper because technically it should have been postponed and then conducted by persons unconnected to the *Bellipotent*. In attacking that view as liberal, Judge Posner contends that in war the legal rules are different, that since there was (in Captain Vere's mind) the genuine fear of a threatened mutiny (a mutiny had been reported on a sister ship), the captain had no choice.

In support of his position, Judge Posner quotes the captain: "Before a court less arbitrary and more merciful than a martial one, that plea [that Billy intended neither mutiny nor homicide] would largely extenuate. At the Last Assizes it shall acquit. But how here? We proceed under the law of the Mutiny Act . . . For that law and the rigor of it, we are not responsible."

On rereading *Billy Budd,* I have been influenced, and greatly so, by my recent reading of another literary military trial, the French court-martial of Privates Didier, Langlois and Ferol, as described in *Paths of Glory* (by Humphrey Cobb, reprinted by the University of Georgia Press). *Paths of Glory* is perhaps the most powerful war novel ever written; the summary conviction and firing-squad end of three innocent men condemns World War I, perhaps all wars, and certainly all courts-martial.

The hint in *Billy Budd* becomes almost unbearable in *Paths of Glory*: a court-martial (at least a literary court-martial) is not just a legal tribunal with uniformed military officers replacing black-robed judges. It seems, rather, to be a farce or a guignol, presided over by Mars himself, a grotesque, unkempt man who always wears an ill-fitting helmet, one that's too large or too small by several sizes.

Civilian judges, even the most insufferable ones, have never insisted that court proceedings must bear their own names; the court-martial, however, pays this very deference to its imperial presiding authority. Perhaps the most disturbing characteristic of these two literary courts-martial was their speed; Billy Budd and the French privates were tried, convicted, and eliminated in a few hours. Mars, with wars to foment all over the globe, is always in a hurry. There is little time for such niceties as due process or cross-examination or appeals. But then no one ever said that the stubble-faced Mars was a civil libertarian.

As the story of Billy Budd begins, the warship *H.M.S. Bellipotent,* heading for the open sea, is pushed off from the anchored British merchantman, *Rights-of-Man* (so christened by its Scottish owner after the book of that name written by Thomas Paine). By the story's end, the

Bellipotent had travelled very far from *Rights* (as she was called). It is suggested here that Melville didn't pick the name of that even more distant ship by chance.

September 15, 1988

Garbage,
the Law,
and Tennessee
Williams

When I was growing up in Brooklyn, Mom did every chore but one; she shopped (it was before freezers, and shopping was a daily task), she cooked, cleaned, did the dishes, made the beds, polished the silver (on those rare occasions when we had company), nursed the sick, encouraged the disappointed, and helped with the homework. But she never once took out the garbage. That obligation fell to my father, and later, as we grew out of infancy, to my brother and to me.

Taking out the garbage meant carrying the pail to the elevator, taking the elevator to the basement (a short enough ride, since we lived on the first floor), and then dumping it in one of two big receptacles that were kept just a few steps away. The elevator was small and creaky and somewhat smelly, since not everyone was as careful as we not to spill. And the basement was always smelly, because the two bins were always brimming; one could never put the garbage *in* the receptacle, but one always tried to balance it on top and to leave instantly so as not to be there when it toppled. If the basement smell was too strong, I would keep one foot in the elevator and toss the contents of our pail toward the bins; in that way

I would not lose the elevator, hence not have to wait in the aromatic cellar for its eventual return.

When I married, my wife assumed all the tasks that Mom had so faithfully discharged but, like Mom, she left the garbage removal to me (or the children). In our Manhattan apartment building, as in most, there is an incinerator room on every floor, so the garbage detail is less taxing. But it is still no honor.

During the Constitutional Bicentennial celebration at the New York County Lawyers' Association, a distinguished panel of scholars and jurists, including a senior federal judge (male), was asked pointed questions about the judiciary. One questioner rose to challenge what was described as the increasing arrogance of judges. The immediate response from the senior federal judge (to whom the remark could not have been directed) was: "I take out the garbage every night."

And so for all these years it has seemed as if men, despite their proud professional, athletic, and business feats, despite their boasting, have been forced to perform society's most menial duty. This apparent anomaly, which has mystified sociologists for generations, has now, for the first time, been explained by the Supreme Court of the United States. As set forth in its recent decision, *California v. Greenwood,* taking out the garbage is, like the power to declare war, a grave constitutional matter. It is too important to be left to women.

The issue in *Greenwood* was whether law-enforcement officials can commandeer a person's garbage, securely wrapped in opaque bags and left on the sidewalk for the usual morning pick-up, without first obtaining a search warrant. It was done to Mr. Greenwood (and the evidence of a drug business was found), who argued that the warrantless tampering violated his constitutional rights under the Fourth Amendment. The lower courts agreed, but the Supreme Court (with two dissents) reversed, ruling that you can have no reasonable claim to privacy once you have "exposed your garbage to the public." Since children, scavengers and dogs routinely have a go at the garbage (argued the Court), why not the cops? The dissent argued that since our garbage contains evidence of our innermost secrets, it is unbecoming for the Government to sniff around as if it (the Government) were a raccoon.

But the purpose of this essay is not to debate the merits of *Greenwood* but, rather, to record the transcendental importance of carrying the day's refuse from kitchen to curb. As I read *Greenwood*, I recalled a scene from *Camino Real*, Tennessee Williams's morality play about our transient roles in this strange but unyielding world. At least it may be about that; there are many interpretations. Two of the play's characters are Street-cleaners, who have no words to speak but who dominate Block (i.e., Chapter) Fourteen. They are coming with their barrel to collect Kilroy himself; Kilroy, as I read the play, stands for us all. And so, as the music grows louder and the Streetcleaners approach, Kilroy, in a frenzy, screams: "COME ON, YOU SONS OF BITCHES! KILROY IS HERE. HE'S READY."

There follows a boxing match between Kilroy and the Streetcleaners, in which Kilroy collapses. But just before he is scooped up and dumped into the waiting bin, he is rescued. For the rest of Kilroy's fate you will have to read Blocks Fifteen and Sixteen. The point here is that in *Camino Real* we (you and I) are (even if metaphorically) the ultimate garbage; it is, perhaps, a modern interpretation of the biblical aphorism that life is a cycle from dust to dust.

Reading *Greenwood v. California* in the light of *Camino Real*, I suppose that choosing sides on the merits of *Greenwood* becomes inevitable. If Tennessee Williams is right, albeit metaphorically, that the ultimate garbage is Man, I hope, at the very least, that the police will need a search warrant before they start poking around. I don't mean to be ghoulish or prim, but I would not want to be handled by one of Attorney General Ed Meese's men without a court order, even posthumously. I'm ticklish.

June 10, 1988

Al and Max
Respectfully
Dissent

When he read the Supreme Court's decision in *Florida v. Bostick*, Ernest Hemingway realized that he would have to make a revision, albeit a small revision, in his short story, *The Killers*.

Toward the middle of the story, while Al and Max, the two hired gunmen, are waiting in Henry's luncheonette for Ole Andreson, their intended victim, Al comes out of the kitchen:

> The cut-off barrels of the shotgun made a slight bulge under the waist of his too tight-fitting overcoat. He straightened his coat with his gloved hands.

That was the sentence, Hemingway thought, that had to be altered if his story were to be consistent with the very latest in legal thinking. Not that his stories always had to mesh perfectly with the law, of course, but this new theory, supported as it was by six justices of the U.S. Supreme Court, simply could not be ignored by a writer who aimed for realism.

Hemingway read the *Bostick* opinion one more time to make sure that he had it just right, because there would be no sense changing the language of a long-ago written piece if it was not absolutely necessary. In that case one Mr. Terrance Bostick was traveling by bus from Miami to

166

Atlanta, and while making a brief stop at Fort Lauderdale, police officers in full uniform, guns in holsters, boarded and asked passengers "for permission to search their luggage." Bostick gave his permission, and the inspection of his luggage uncovered cocaine. The issue before the Court was whether the search, being without any warrant, was constitutional. The case turned on whether Bostick's consent had been given freely or had been coerced. The nicety that the Court focused on—both in the majority opinion and in the dissent—was whether pistols residing in policemen's holsters constituted coercion, or whether, for there to be coercion, those pistols had to be brandished in your nose. The majority opinion held that since "the officers did not point guns at Bostick," his agreement to let them examine his luggage had not been coerced. The majority concluded that since no gun had been pointed at Bostick's head, he was free to refuse permission and even free to leave the bus (although his luggage, stored below, would have traveled to Atlanta without him).

After reviewing the decision, Hemingway was sure that he had to change the language quoted above, the language about the bulge of the shotgun under Al's coat, because the necessary implication of that sentence was that the mere sight of the gun's bulge constituted a threat to the viewer, even though the gun itself was pointed at no one. That necessary implication, Hemingway realized, had now been undercut by no less an authority than the U.S. Supreme Court, as reflected in its *Bostick* decision. As he pondered revised language, language that would be consistent with the law of the land, both Al and Max, the two hired assassins, objected. Al spoke:

> Mr. Hemingway, please don't change one word. Whatever those judges may say, let me tell you that we've gotten plenty of mileage out of just showing the outlines of our little shotgun, just letting some guy see that we've got a bulge. When me or Max or one of our boys shows up with this kind of bulge in our coats, the other guy always turns over the money. This kind of bulge has worked miracles in banks, gas stations, liquor stores and just last week in a vehicle operated by Brinks, if you know what I mean.

Mr. Hemingway replied:

Max and Al, let me explain that what you just described all happened before the Supreme Court rendered its opinion in *Florida v. Bostick*. From now on nobody will be coerced by some bulge under your coat. People will probably assume that it's only a clarinet. Unless you point the shotgun between their eyes, people will no longer be coerced into doing anything that they don't want to do.

Max replied:

Mr. Hemingway, we are suggesting to you, on the authority of Al's bulge, that you leave that sentence alone. Now if you really believe that the Supreme Court knows what it is doing, you'll make the change because we ain't pointing our little weapon at you or at anybody else. But if you pick up your pen to make some change we ain't responsible for the consequences. And let us both repeat that this ain't no coercion. You're free to make, or not to make, any change you want. After all, it's your short story.

Mr. Hemingway pondered his two choices. On the one hand, based on the Supreme Court's reasoning in *Bostick,* he had nothing to fear; on the other hand, he remembered the fate of Francis Macomber, the principal character in his own short story, *The Short Happy Life of Francis Macomber,* who was blown away by a shotgun blast. Weighing his two alternatives, Mr. Hemingway decided, strictly on the basis of his own free and uncoerced will, to leave the story unchanged.

July 31, 1991

'Palsgraf,' a One-Act Drama

Palsgraf v. The Long Island Railroad Company, a landmark decision in the law, was written by Chief Justice Benjamin Cardozo of the New York Court of Appeals. But that was an inadvertence. It should have been written by Samuel Beckett or Eugene Ionesco or Luigi Pirandello because *Palsgraf* (its nom de theatre) is not a legal matter at all. It is, rather, a one-act drama in the theater of the absurd.

The facts, as duly reported at 248 New York Reports 339 (1928), were these: A woman, by all accounts an ordinary woman, one Helen Palsgraf, had purchased a railroad ticket for passage to Rockaway Beach. While waiting patiently at the far end of the platform for her train, another train, with a different destination, arrived. It lingered for a few moments, discharging and accepting passengers, and then the doors closed and it resumed its voyage. As it was leaving the station, picking up speed, two latecomers raced to climb aboard. One, with a marvelous leap, made it; but the other man, less nimble, faltered. That by itself could be a metaphor for life itself, how some make it and some don't, but we are concerned here with only the essential facts as detailed at 248 New York Reports, not with sentimental detours. The faltering traveler was helped by two railroad guards, one on board and one on the plat-

169

form. In the course of helping the tottering rider, a small newspaper-wrapped package that he was carrying became dislodged. Such an event would usually be too trivial even for a court of law to note, but that particular newspaper-wrapped package was a package of July 4th fireworks. And when it fell to the ground it exploded, and the shock waves knocked down several scales that chanced to be located at the same far end of the platform where one Helen Palsgraf, an ordinary person from all that appears, was patiently standing while awaiting the expected arrival of the local to Rockaway Beach. As the scales fell they fell, of course, right upon the innocent Ms. Palsgraf, who suffered some rather nasty cuts and bruises. No puns will be used here to suggest that those scales were metaphors for the scales of justice, although such a play on words would be appropriate because when Helen Palsgraf sued the Long Island Railroad Company for her injuries, she lost. She lost to Chief Judge Cardozo's reasoning that the railroad was not responsible because Ms. Palsgraf's injuries were not foreseeable: ". . . there was nothing in the situation to suggest to the most cautious mind that the parcel wrapped in newspaper would spread wreckage through the station."

And with that bit of judicial logic—i.e., that there could be no recovery because her injury could not have been reasonably foreseen by the reasonable guards—the famous legal case of *Palsgraf v. The Long Island Railroad Company* ends. And just there, at that instant, at that flickering instant, the theater of the absurd begins:

> *Ms. Helen Palsgraf (a woman, neatly dressed, in her mid-40's):* Your Honor, if I would have foreseen the accident I would not have stood at the end of the platform surrounded by heavy scales. So the fact that I did not foresee the danger is precisely why I was hurt. It's backwards of you to say, therefore, that that is why I should not recover.
>
> *Judge (grim-faced in his black magisterial robes):* The reason that I decided your case as I did is that I did not foresee that excellent argument.
>
> *Ms. Palsgraf:* Your Honor, why does the law depend on something as vague, as subjective, as meaningless as foreseeability?

Judge: That is a question, frankly, that I did not foresee.

Ms. Palsgraf: I suggest that linking legal liability with foreseeability creates two classes of citizens. Prophets, for instance, can look into the future better than others. Are prophets, therefore, held to a higher standard? And if so, how do we know who is, and who is not, a prophet. Is there some kind of test?

Judge: Frankly, Ms. Palsgraf, that's another point that I had not foreseen.

Ms. Palsgraf: What this discussion does prove, with all due respect, your Honor, is that you, Sir, are not a prophet.

Judge (unhappy to hear any diminution of his stature): I could, with one snap of my judicial fingers, make myself a prophet or anything else. All I have to do is sign an order. But if I made myself a prophet I'd have to pay income taxes, particularly because I am so impeccably neat. Making a tidy prophet always causes problems with the Internal Revenue people.

Ms. Palsgraf: If it's too costly to be a prophet, why don't you become an oracle. In that way you would still be able to foresee things, but you'd save the taxes.

Judge: I could, of course, snap my judicial fingers and become an oracle, just like that. But it would hurt my advancement up the judicial scale if I were known as a bleeding heart. So I cannot become either an oracle or a ventricle.

Ms. Palsgraf: Your Honor, doesn't it affect your ability as a judge if you are neither a prophet nor an oracle? Would you not be more effective if you were able to foresee some of the consequences of your decisions?

Judge: Now *that's* a good question. But it shows that you don't understand how the legal system works. Let me explain it. Because the law is based on precedent, nothing new ever happens. The law pushes forward by not moving, by not moving even one inch. Therefore foresight and hindsight are identical. So there is no need to be a prophet or an oracle; it's a waste of time. All I have to do if I want to see into the future is to open my eyes and do an about-face.

Ms. Palsgraf: If foreseeability is just a charade, why did I not recover in my lawsuit against the Long Island Railroad? Why didn't I win?
Judge: Because it didn't matter whether you were going to or coming from Rockaway Beach. Frontwards and backwards are the same. The law is not bogged down in details.
Ms. Palsgraf: Your Honor, your comment raises some very serious questions.

As the curtain begins to drop slowly, the scene switches to a conversation in Samuel Beckett's *Endgame,* in which Clove says to Hamm (or is it some judge speaking?):
All life long the same questions, the same answers.
Finis.

November 21, 1991

Borders

I.

If the borders of the United States were pushed in, as were the borders in Eugene Ionesco's drama, *Exit The King*, the Nation would be reduced to a few square miles in southern Iowa. It is not clear why the borders in *Exit The King* were squeezed together. Perhaps to mock the very idea of a monarchy, for as King Berenger died the borders of his mythical state collapsed with him. Perhaps to mock at the very idea of borders, for borders artificially, but effectively, separate people. Perhaps the meaning of the play is even more symbolic, suggesting that when any of us dies everything we are dies with us, except perhaps our good name. I added the good name reservation on my own—I don't think it is suggested in the play—for if not even a good name survives, what's the point of living an honorable life? As kings go, Berenger was neither all good nor all bad (on the same page it was said of him: "He was gentle, he was tender"; and "Really quite wicked. Revengeful and cruel"). And it was concluded that, on balance, he would be remembered hardly at all ("He will be a page in a book of ten thousand pages in one of a million libraries which has a million books").

If, like King Berenger's mythical state, the borders of the United States were to collapse, leaving only a four-square mile principality in southern Iowa, gone forever would be the Statue of Liberty (at the Statue's centennial celebration in 1986 the fireworks were stupendous), the Golden Gate Bridge, Ebbets Field, the Sears Tower, Carnegie Hall (as reupholstered), the Capitol in D.C., Neiman Marcus, the Rose Bowl,

173

the Space Needle in Seattle, Interstate 95, the Library of Congress, the Shoreham Nuclear Plant, Dodger Stadium, the Mayo Clinic, the Chicago Art Institute, the Holland Tunnel, Fort Knox, Wrigley Field, Boston Garden, and the Haitian refugee problem. The Haitian refugee problem would disappear because, the United States being a landlocked principality a thousand miles from the sea, there would be no United States shoreline toward which the refugees could set sail.

II.

Article 1.2 of the United Nations Protocol Relating to the Status of Refugees defines a "refugee" as a person absent from his country due to a "well founded fear of being persecuted for reasons of race, religion, nationality, [or] membership of a particular social group or political opinion." And there's the rub, because the Haitian refugees are victims of a democratic tyranny which kills people indiscriminately, without regard to their "race, religion, nationality, [or] membership of a particular social group or political opinion." An article in the New York Times of December 25, 1991 (beginning at p. 1) describes Haiti's "atmosphere of violence," "a 'scorched earth policy' . . . that had been used by the army to terrorize a population that continues to ask for Father Aristide's [the deposed president] return," and "'the homicidal character of [Haiti's] political culture.'" To escape that all-pervasive (albeit random and democratic) terror, Haitians did what terror victims have been doing for over two centuries—they risked all to head to the United States.

III.

Because they are victims of a non-discriminatory terror, the Haitians are not "refugees," so back they are sent. To them the United States has shriveled to a landlocked, four-square mile principality in southern Iowa. Gone is the Statue of Liberty. At the Statue's centennial celebration in

1986 the fireworks were stupendous. As *Exit The King* ends, Queen Marguerite, continuing her soliloquy, says: "It was a lot of fuss about nothing, wasn't it."

January 7, 1992

VIII
Two Essays
on the Law
and Russia

A Russian
Fantasy

An American law firm (Coudert Brothers of New York) opened an office in Moscow; glasnost, like Humpty Dumpty, had taken one step too many. All the commissar's horses and all the commissar's apparatchiks were not able to put the Soviet Union back together again. Although the bar association likes to believe that the USSR disintegrated because those brave Americans carried with them our Constitution and preached its liberties with a missionary zeal, the truth is less heroic.

It seems that the one thing every law firm needs is lawyers, and so an equal-opportunity want-ad was duly placed in *Pravda*, seeking inexperienced beginners at the "going rate" of $75,000 (U.S.) per year. And Russia was never the same.

The Revolution that began in 1917 (when all the soldiers at the front just abandoned the trenches and walked home) ended after a pretty eventful run of some 70 years (when all the people just abandoned their jobs to go to law school). Stakhanovites who had mined 10 tons of coal a day with their bare hands left the pits, bureaucrats and technocrats left their desks, and farmers abandoned the fields. They were immediately joined by chess players with winning positions and chess players about to resign, by army officers stationed in Afghanistan and corporals on Warsaw Pact maneuvers in Hungary, and by party ideologists who could shift feet if they had to.

179

Western diplomats reported that the movement—the avalanche—to law school seemed to include everyone: ballet stars from the Kirov and ballerinas in tutus from the provinces, Raisa Gorbachev (she wanted to lower the import duties on smocks from Givenchy), spacemen in those funny suits, KGB enforcers (if they didn't get scholarships they promised some original cross-examination of the dean), soccer and hockey players, Svetlana Stalin (they were saying unkind things about dad and she wanted to study the laws of libel and slander), circus clowns and high-wire daredevils, yogurt-eating octagenarians from the Ukraine and their parents, Pushkin scholars and Trotsky debunkers, gymnasts, vodka drinkers, worshipers at St. Basil's, Voice of America jammers, borsht (with sour cream) bottlers, Romanov pretenders (they were going to study the laws of descent; perhaps they could be restored to the throne, or at least to a palace), trainers of dancing bears, guards from the Gulag, prisoners from the Gulag (law school might be dull, but it would be an improvement), Hermitage curators, Volga boatmen, Aeroflot steward-esses, mathematicians (if you start at $75,000 a year and win increases of 6.5 percent compounded annually. . .), Battle of Stalingrad veterans (hoping that the G.I. Bill was still operative), ICBM aimers (if they didn't get scholarships it was goodbye to the law school, and to the build-ings on either side), May Day revelers, *Izvestia* obituary writers, Men-shevik survivers (they planned to specialize in lost causes), samizdat press distributors (they always needed a lawyer), refuseniks, samovar polishers, Helsinki Treaty Watchers (they always needed a lawyer), weight lifters, kulaks, pianists from the Tchaikovsky Competition and violinists from Odessa (hoping for upscale salaries), and the last balalaika player in Chernobyl (business was slow; people weren't dancing anymore).

Joining them, and ending the Revolution officially, were poets from St. Petersburg.

February 25, 1988

East
and
West

Vaclav Havel was sent to prison because he opposed
Communism and Eugene Dennis was sent to prison
because he favored Communism, which proves that
Columbus may have been right after all—this world, indeed, may be
circular.

This past summer I saw a production of Havel's one-act play, *Audience*.
It is an encounter between Czechoslovakia's mythical playwright, Ferdinand Vanek, and a nameless brewmaster (who is also a functionary in
the Czech Communist Party). The brewmaster-functionary is under
constant pressure from the higher-ups to report on various employees,
including, particularly, Vanek the playwright. To his credit, the brewmaster, a vulgar but otherwise not bad fellow, is uncomfortable with the
snooping. "I'm runnin' outta ideas about what to keep on tellin' 'em
every damn week—I really don't know the first thing about you."

As a solution, the brewmaster hits upon a novel idea—he proposes
that Vanek himself undertake the task of making the weekly reports. But
Vanek refuses, "I can't be snitching on myself."

The play's punch comes from the wonderful circularity, the ridicu-
lousness of asking a man to spy on himself. No wonder they put Havel

in jail. But, of course, it didn't matter. The message got through, and the regime was overthrown.

And circularity is also the key to understanding *United States v. Dennis*. The United States once had a law, the Smith Act, that made it a crime to advocate the overthrow of our government by force and violence. A group of Communists, including the head of the party in the United States, one Eugene Dennis, was indicted under the Act, and tried and convicted. It was in the late 1940s, after World War II, during the cold war; to place events in context, the Soviets were blockading Berlin and the world was edgy. The legal issue was whether the Smith Act, which outlawed mere advocacy (albeit of force and violence), violated the First Amendment's guarantee of free speech. Although the *Dennis* case reached the U.S. Supreme Court (which upheld the convictions, 7-2), the most important decision was written in the Court of Appeals by Judge Learned Hand (considered by many to be one of the most outstanding jurists of his time). Judge Hand's opinion in *Dennis* is long and includes much Latin (pro tanto, vàde mecum, status quo, modus vivendi, corruptio optimi pessima, laissez faire and a fortiori) and a little Greek (a passing reference to Zeus's son, Rhadamanthus). At the core of the opinion's logic is this simple, circular aphorism, "Revolutions are often 'right,' but a 'right of revolution' is a contradiction in terms . . ."

Can an American judge really have ruled that you can be sent to jail for doing something that is often "right"? And if so, where do they send the people who do wrong?

And, upon analysis, the *Dennis* opinion becomes even more confusing. The traditional test under our Constitution of whether dangerous-sounding speech is allowed is whether it poses "a clear and present danger." That means that speech is legal as long as it is inept, but advocacy with a bite might break the law. The qualification about "force and violence" is, I suggest, just a legalism, because the pen really is mightier than the sword, and the satire of a Vaclav Havel has a much greater chance of stirring a popular revolution in the streets than the wooden "sacred texts" of a Eugene Dennis. The hard question of this essay therefore is: How would Judge Learned Hand have ruled had he been hearing an appeal from Vaclav Havel's conviction and jail sentence? Don't scoff.

Don't be so sure. Think about it. Weren't Havel's words, like Dennis's, meant to stir the people to action, meant to overthrow the government?

Columbus sailed from Spain and crossed the Atlantic in search of India, proving that East and West were the same navigationally. *Dennis* suggests that in the cold war era East and West may have also been the same jurisprudentially, caelum di meliora, Heaven forbid. Columbus I knew about; the Latin I had to look up.

October 12, 1990

IX
American
History

It's a
Grand
Old Flag

Several of the Supreme Court opinions in *Texas v. Johnson* (the flag-burning case) sound like film clips from *Yankee Doodle Dandy*. The expressed views of Chief Justice Rehnquist and Justices Kennedy and Stevens seem to be hoofing with Jimmy Cagney through "Over There" and "You're a Grand Old Flag." But all the opinions in the case (including Justice Brennan's, with which I agree) have, I suggest, missed the point, to wit, that all American flags are not alike, at least not alike for First Amendment purposes. The flags that the justices wrote about so passionately included all the great ones: the flag celebrated in Ralph Waldo Emerson's "Concord Hymn," the flag for which Barbara Frietchie offered her "old gray head," and the flags raised by the bravest of men at Iwo Jima, Bataan and Omaha Beach. But the flag that Gregory Lee Johnson (of *Texas v. Johnson*) desecrated was of a less sacred cloth; it was a flag burned to protest the 1984 Republican National Convention in Dallas. There are American flags and there are American flags, and all are not as noble as the Court's honored symbols; this essay will discuss three of the less worthy ones in an attempt to put the matter into some perspective.

There is the flag of fickle patriotism that appears, almost incidentally, in the record of the *Trial of the Lincoln Conspirators* (1865). One of the alleged conspirators, Mrs. Mary E. Surratt (the only woman so charged), was accused of having harbored the whole gang of murderers and plotters and to have hidden their weapons in a back room above the loft. One of those called to testify in her defense was a Mr. J. Z. Jenkins. To prove his own veracity and loyalty to the Republic he testified as follows:

> In 1861, about the time of the first Bull Run fight, I got a United States flag from Washington, which I and several of our neighbors raised. There came a report shortly after that it was going to be taken down by secesh sympathizers. I went round the neighborhood and collected some 20 or 30 men with muskets, double-barreled guns, or whatever they had, and we lay all night round the flag to keep it up. I was there one night and a day, I think.

Despite his self-serving testimony about his devotion to the flag, Mr. Jenkins was thoroughly discredited and proven to be disloyal. And, parenthetically, Mrs. Surratt was found guilty and was sentenced to hang. The flag at the Conspirators' Trial represents, at best, a passing patriotism, most unlike the flags cited by the Court in *Johnson*.

The saddest of American flags that I know of is the one recounted in the Yiddish poem *Salute* (1934) by Moyshe-Leyb Halpern; it is about a lynching. I do not read or speak Yiddish, and both the original text and the translation appear in *American Yiddish Poetry, A Bilingual Anthology* (University of California Press, 1986). One stanza reads:

> But not only did they loop a rope
> Around the neck of this piece of cattle,
> The flag of the republic too
> Was raised on high—
> And the sky was blue—it didn't care—
> And the wind rejoiced with the flag in the air,
> And I—a beaten dog—said not a word.
> Took no part, a partner to murder.

Whether any justice of the High Court would deem the burning of *that* flag to be a crime I cannot say; but I suggest that it is not a flag that invokes the heroic patriotic muse.

The crassest flag—one described as a "unique full-sized American flag"—is the one soon to be dedicated by Senator Don Nickles for all members of "George Bush's Republican Presidential Task Force." One can obtain the flag by sending the Task Force $120 (either in full or in 12 monthly installments); it is described as "a replica of the one presented to Ronald Reagan upon his stepping down from the Presidency of the United States." If you pay that $120 you not only receive a "unique" flag, but official Republican Party thanks for helping to defeat "extremist" "ultra-liberal" Senate Democrats in 1990. If that Task Force flag is "unique," doesn't it necessarily mean that it is not the same flag that flutters over Mount Suribachi?

As I write this essay I have thought back to when I first saw *Yankee Doodle Dandy*. It was at the Vogue Theater, a local movie house on Coney Island Avenue, just off Avenue K in Brooklyn. And I can still see that funny walk—more like a march—that Jimmy Cagney had as he tap-danced and sang all those wonderful George M. Cohan melodies. "Give My Regards to Broadway" was my favorite, and sometimes I hum it still. I can't quite place it in time, but I guess that it was in the 1940s. I remember how much I enjoyed that movie, and I think I'd like it just as much now. It was—and is—great. It's just not a very good guide for Constitutional law.

July 21, 1989

An Election
Year (1988)
Fable

George Mason favored the Bill of Rights and opposed slavery, and that cost him the presidential election in 1988. It's too bad, too, because, with the possible exception of Thomas Jefferson, he was the most qualified candidate ever.

He was not only telegenic (some said he looked like Clark Gable so that the women's vote was virtually guaranteed), but his qualifications for the presidency were a media man's dream: he was one of the most successful planters in the Colonies, a vestryman in Truro Parish, a Fairfax County Justice, a trustee of Alexandria, and a member of the Virginia House of Burgesses. He wrote the Fairfax Resolves in 1774 (which set forth, more clearly than ever before, the Colonies' constitutional position for independence); and, in 1776, as a delegate to the Virginia Constitutional Convention, he drafted the Virginia Declaration of Rights (which formed the basis, a few months later, of the Declaration of Independence). James Madison said of him that he possessed "the greatest talents for debate of any man he had ever seen or heard speak." There was certainly reason for guarded optimism at Mason headquarters as Campaign '88 began.

But then, just before the Iowa primary—the polls showed him leading with 85 percent of the vote—came the shattering revelation about his past that forced George Mason out of the race and into political obscurity. Just 201 years earlier, as a delegate to the Constitutional Convention, Mason had voted *against* the adoption of our Constitution. At first, that 1787 vote was mentioned casually and in whispers by this or that political opponent; then it was referred to more frequently and more loudly in those vague press briefings given by vague people who are vaguely described as this or that politician's spokesperson; then it appeared on bumper stickers on millions and millions of automobiles; then it worked its way into that new forum for meaningful political discourse, the 15-second TV spot; then the message was announced by so many red-white-and-blue posters that not one brown telephone pole was still visible in the land; leaflets, reminding Americans of Mason's vote, replaced the Sunday newspaper as the world's largest source of waste paper; from coast to coast editorials became caustic ("How can a man be expected to defend the Constitution when he himself voted against it?"); and television comics had a field day ("What do George Mason and high cholesterol have in common? Both are bad for your constitution." Yuk yuk yuk).

Finally, the message picked up such momentum, that much of the nation, in a frenzy, seemed to yell it into one enormous bullhorn: GEORGE MASON OPPOSED THE CONSTITUTION! The reverberation was so great that geological plates shifted, causing earthquakes from Maine to Hawaii.

But the epicenter of the storm was in the election campaign, where it registered a 10 on the political Richter scale. George Mason's negative ratings rose to 100 percent (with no margin of error), funds dried up, and his campaign ended. Some political analysts said that what did George Mason in was not only the startling revelation that he had voted against our Constitution, but that he was not contrite. "I'd vote that way again today," he said quietly but defiantly as he closed his Dubuque headquarters, surrounded by hundreds of angry, yelling Iowans, many with placards that proclaimed in red-white-and-blue: GEORGE MASON OPPOSED THE CONSTITUTION!

Many years later, an enterprising young reporter, who was researching past presidential elections for a TV special, chanced to interview George Mason on the porch of his home in Alexandria, Va. Mr. Mason spoke reflectively about the most stunning political shift in history, the shift that had shattered his presidential hopes: "No, I'm not bitter," he said. "That's the way the political game was played." In response to a question as to why he had voted against the Constitution, Mason brought out a copy of James Madison's *Notes of Debates in the Federal Convention of 1787* and said, simply, "It's all there, young man, for anyone to read."

The reporter could not believe that George Mason's "No" vote had been a matter of public record for over two centuries, because it had burst onto the 1988 campaign as if it had been newly discovered evidence. Ignoring how his opponent had used his "No" vote in the 1988 Campaign, the Virginia patriarch explained exactly how it happened back there in 1787:

"I remember it well, as if it were yesterday. As the Convention was about to close, ol' Ben Franklin rose to speak, but his age and his arthritis got the better of him, and he handed his speech to his fellow Pennsylvanian, James Wilson. It was a beautiful speech, too, one of which Ben was justifiably proud. At the end of his remarks, Ben said—that is Wilson said it, although Ben had written in—that we should vote for the Constitution unanimously because—and these are the exact words—'because I expect no better, and because I am not sure that it is not the best.' As soon as Wilson finished, he sat down and I asked to be recognized, which of course I was. I told the assembled delegates—friends one and all—that I had the highest respect for Ben but that I couldn't vote for a constitution that did not include a Bill of Rights and that sanctioned slavery. I said that I expected better even if Ben didn't. I told the delegates that if we included a Bill of Rights and abolished slavery we would have written the best constitution in the history of the world, that we had come so far that we ought not sign off just before our real work was done.

"Well, it was getting late on that Monday, Sept. 17, 1787. We'd been in Philadelphia since May and, I suppose, folks were wearing out. Then Ben Franklin made his talk, and said that that was about the best we could do so let's adopt it, and the delegates found it too easy to agree.

Franklin was, after all, one of the most liberal men at the Convention, so people argued that if it was good enough for Ben it should be good enough for the rest of us. But I voted 'No,' and I'd vote 'No' again today if the same issues were before me.

"By the way, I wasn't the only 'No' vote. I recall there were several, including Elbridge Gerry of Massachusetts. I guess they were liberal in Massachusetts even then."

Just then the reporter broke in: "Mr. Mason, why didn't you explain all that back in 1988? It would have saved your candidacy. You would have been elected President of the United States."

George Mason rocked a few times on his rocker, and then replied:

"I did young man, I did. I explained it a dozen times, but I was drowned out by all the din and those one-sentence commercials and those ubiquitous red-white-and-blue posters. The campaign of 1988 was still the political winter, and the voice of the turtle was not yet heard in the land."

September 22, 1988

A Precedent
Worth Considering

Although he was one of the original members of Phi Beta Kappa (College of William and Mary, Class of 1778), a member of the Virginia legislature, a member of the Virginia convention that adopted (in 1788) the United States Constitution, and an unusually popular person, his uncle, George Washington, appointed him to no office. But Bushrod Washington was so highly thought of that President John Adams nominated him (in 1798) as his first choice for the United States Supreme Court, before even the revered John Marshall (whom President Adams chose later).

This essay reflects on whether President George Bush should have nominated his first cousin, District Judge John Walker, to a vacancy on the Court of Appeals for the Second Circuit. There are, to be sure, many advantages in having a President nominate his family members for high federal office:

1. One's relatives usually represent a surprisingly broad social and political spectrum. Embarrassingly, every family has a few well-meaning iconoclasts, a few individualists, a few malcontents, and their presence in our otherwise dull government is bound to produce a touch of desperately needed irreverence. In almost every prior administration, jobs were filled only by the ideologically pure. Hence President Bush's same-tribe-only technique is not only innovative, but liberating.

2. As the word gets out across the land that those on the White

House genealogy chart have the inside track, millions of Americans will be able to go back to what they like doing best, whether it is reading poetry or tending their gardens. In prior administrations those people spent all their spare time (and more) in currying favor.

3. There has been, particularly in recent years, some harsh criticism that our courts are no longer collegial. With all judges being related to the President, hence to each other, a new level of harmony will prevail and magistrates will be able to spend all their time on jurisprudential issues rather than on personal, but unseemly, squabbles.

4. Substantial sums will be saved on judicial conventions. Henceforth they can all be held, just before the dessert, at the family's Thanksgiving Dinner.

5. Funds now squandered on those pointless FBI "background checks" can be rerouted, instead, to save a few of those Texas savings and loans.

6. Lower court judges, who once eyed the glories of higher and higher benches, will no longer be tempted to decide cases with an eye to the political ramifications. My guess is that, as a result, courts, too, will become kinder and gentler places, and fairer.

7. The perennial pressure for government pay raises will end and judges will (finally) stop wailing about some first-year lawyers who earn as much as they. For if the pay scale is askew, the fault will not be the Congress's, but in judges' genes.

Against all of these tangible advantages of nominating members of the presidential clan for high office there is but one disadvantage, the disadvantage of public cynicism. That is doubtless what motivated President Washington, a most devoted family man, to bypass his favorite nephew. But when President Adams nominated Bushrod Washington for the Supreme Court, his famous uncle congratulated the new nominee in a most felicitous letter (at Vol. 36, *The Writings of George Washington,* p. 519):

> I wish your Circuit may be pleasant and honorable to you and that you may return safe to your family and friends.

A George Washington precedent is always a good precedent to follow.

Which means, in this case, that George Bush should, of course, send a hearty congratulatory note to any of his kinsmen who may some day chance to be nominated for a high federal office. But the nomination itself should be left, most discreetly, to the wisdom of another President.

November 13, 1989

Of
Maize
and
Zucchini

T here would be no need to fret about New York State's unexpected projected budget deficit of $1.9 billion (for the fiscal year ending March 31, 1989) if the U.S. Court of Appeals for the Second Circuit (Foley Square, New York City) had correctly decided the Oneida Indian Nation case. If that case (discussed below) had been correctly decided, the State would be so flush that a deficit of a billion dollars or two would be handled by the loose change in its petty cash box; indeed, the State would also be able to pay off the entire federal government deficit (estimated at $2.5 trillion), build the Pentagon's dream 600-ship navy (and make them all aircraft carriers, if that's what the admirals want for Christmas), and still have enough money left over to pay Orel Hershiser the salary that talented man deserves. But the three-judge federal panel wrongly decided *Oneida* and, instead of those few luxuries, the State of New York will suffer a dreary freeze on wages and hiring.

Oneida involves the sale in 1785 (the Treaty of Fort Herkimer) and 1788 (the Treaty of Fort Schuyler), of 5.3 million acres of land by several Indian tribes to New York State. For that vast tract of their homeland (it is a 60-mile swath that goes from Pennsylvania to Canada), New York State paid the Indians a total consideration of $27,000.*

The litigation began when, a few years ago, the Indians asked for their homeland back and the State of New York refused. The Indians' legal argument, perhaps a bit tardy, was this: The original land sales were null and void because they were not approved by the Continental Congress, as was required (the Indians contend) by the Articles of Confederation. The Articles of Confederation were invoked because the United States Constitution had not yet been ratified. The Circuit Court analyzed the relevant clauses of the Articles of Confederation [Articles IX (1) and (4)], the relevant provisions of the Treaty of Fort Stanwix (by which the new nation made peace with the Indians in 1784), together with the contemporaneous writings of James Madison and Thomas Jefferson, and concluded that those land transactions did not require separate Congressional approval, hence were valid. And so New York keeps the land and the Indian tribes keep the consideration.

Had the decision gone the other way (which it should have; see below), the Indians would have their 5.3 million-acre homeland back (quite valuable at today's land prices), and New York State would have back its $27,000, with appropriate and equitable interest. Since the Indians (in 1785 and 1788) could have (and may have) invested that money in some local savings account or mutual fund or perhaps a 200-year CD, they would have to return that appreciated sum to New York in exchange for the return of their appreciated property. A general, conservative rule of thumb is that properly invested money, if untaxed (there was no U.S. income tax until 1916; and the Indians were exempt anyway), doubles every seven years. Hence, if their homelands were returned, the tribes, in exchange, would pay the State $7.24 trillion.

But the *Oneida* case should have been decided in favor of the Indians not because of financial considerations but because it would be right. A people (whether Iroquois, Oneida, Mohawk, Tuscarora, Israeli, Irish or Armenian) and its land are indivisible. New York State could no more

---

*The precise consideration was $17,000 on the barrel-head, plus $600 a year in perpetuity; that annual payment was discharged by a lump-sum payment in 1839. It is estimated that the total value of the consideration, measured as of 1788, was $27,000.

buy the Indians' homelands in 1785 than Japan, for instance, could buy all the counties of New York State today, even if it were to give all residents the right to vote (albeit for members of the Diet).

But we do not need a hypothetical example to understand the bonding of people to place. The point is made most sharply and most beautifully in Providence, Rhode Island, in the marvelously restored Italian Quarter known as Federal Hill. Where Depasquale and Atwells Avenues intersect there is a piazza; it is no larger than an acre, and is bounded on the north by a Rite-Aid Pharmacy and on the south by Tuscano's Restaurant. Affixed to the side of the pharmacy, facing the open space, are two brass plaques. One plaque tells us:

> On This Location Stood
> The Fruit Stand of
> Sebastian Muratore
> Circa 1930 to 1962
> "My Father, with
> Qualities of Gold"
> Joseph R. Muratore
> March 10, 1979

The second plaque states:

> On This Location Stood
> The Fruit Stand of
> Francesco Garofalo
> and
> His Sons Leo and Joseph
> Circa 1930 to 1960
> "This Was Their Life"
> Leonard A. Garofalo
> 1979

If only the learned *Oneida* judges had understood what Joseph Muratore and Leonard Garofalo understood—that zucchini and tomatoes might be for sale, but never one's place, one's heritage.

November 28, 1988

Perhaps They Should Have Listened to the Mayor of New Haven

The Korean War, the Vietnam War, the invasion of Grenada, the invasion of Panama, and the Persian Gulf Expeditionary Force poised to restore the Emir of Kuwait to his rightful jewel-studded throne might all have been avoided had they listened to Roger Sherman, then the mayor of New Haven.

On Monday, Aug. 6, 1787, Mr. John Rutledge (of South Carolina), chairman of the drafting committee of the Constitutional Convention, delivered his report and circulated to each member a printed draft of a proposed constitution. Article VII, Sec. 1 of that version gave to the Congress, among its many other powers, the specific power "to make war." On Wednesday, Aug. 15, 1787, the assembled delegates discussed that war power, whereupon Mr. James Madison (of Virginia) and Mr. Elbridge Gerry (of Massachusetts)

> moved to insert *declare*, striking out *make* war, leaving to the Executive the power to repel sudden attacks.

And so began a 15-line, three-minute discussion that may have changed much American history two centuries later. For had the Congress's power not been altered, had it remained as the power "to make war," the presidents' (being Presidents Truman, Kennedy, Johnson,

Nixon, Reagan and Bush) favorite legal argument (to wit, that while only Congress could declare a war, there was no constitutional reason why the Chief Executive could not, on his own, launch a war, fight a war, make a war, win a war, join a war, unleash a war, engage in war, or prosecute a war, all to the ultimate victory, so help us God) would not exist.

When delegates Madison and Gerry offered their amendment, Mr. Roger Sherman (of Connecticut), then the mayor of New Haven, opposed the change, arguing that

> The Executive should be able to repel and not to commence war. *Make* is better than *declare*, the latter narrowing the power too much.

And the brief debate that followed put the dimension of the war power into sharp focus. Mr. Gerry, one of the amendment's sponsors, responded to Mr. Sherman's point by commenting that he "never expected to hear in a republic a motion to empower the Executive alone to declare war." Which prompted Mr. Rufus King (of Massachusetts) to note for the record that he favored the amendment because to "make" war could be understood to mean to "conduct" war, and that was, surely, an Executive function. Then Mr. George Mason (of Virginia) rose, and stated that he, too, was against "giving the power of war to the Executive because [it] could not safely be trusted with it." Mr. Mason said that he favored "clogging rather than facilitating war," hence he "preferred *declare* to *make* [war]." The Madison-Gerry amendment passed, with only New Hampshire voting against, Massachusetts abstaining. After several other drafts, Congress's exclusive power "to declare war" became part of Article 1 Section 8.

The transcript of the Constitutional Convention, kept by Mr. James Madison, makes it clear that when the word "declare" was substituted for "make," it was the unanimous intent of the Convention *not* to give the Executive the power to "make" war without a *prior* Congressional declaration of war, except to repel an invasion. For as Mr. George Mason noted, requiring the Congress to "declare war" first meant that the Government would have to deliberate on the issue very carefully, thereby "clogging war," in the hope that, by the deliberative delay, no war would ever have to be "made." It never occurred to any delegate in Philadelphia that by defining Congress's power as the power "to declare war" instead of "to make war" some future president would argue that he, as president, therefore could, unilaterally, "make war."

Since the original intent of the Founding Fathers is as clear as the ultramarine waters of the Persian Gulf, one wonders where are the strict constructionists? They all seem to favor presidentially-authorized wars, relying, apparently, on Article II, Section 2 of the Constitution, which designates the President as the Commander in Chief. Because this is a factual essay only, I do not mean to engage in argument. But since *someone* has to be the commander in chief, the fact that the president is the commander in chief does not seem, logically, to have anything to do with the war power. That is, if a commander in chief, any commander in chief, could nullify the Congress's exclusive power over war just by virtue of being the commander in chief, the Congress's war power wouldn't be much of a power, and the Constitution wouldn't be much of a constitution. The position of the strict constructionists is hard to understand.

According to press reports, 45 members of the House of Representatives have filed a lawsuit challenging President Bush's power to launch an offensive strike against Iraq without first obtaining Congressional approval. As the newspaper article also notes, similar lawsuits in the past have always failed, and no one expects the new litigation to do any better. And the fact that there are now more strict constructionist judges on the bench than ever before does not seem to matter. Au contraire.

In justification of their asserted power "to make war," recent presidents have argued that it is a power that inheres in the presidency itself, and that, therefore, it is a power that has been enjoyed by all prior chief executives. But that argument is too glib, too all-inclusive, because at least one president, one Commander in Chief, would have stoutly disagreed. For before he became the first president of the United States, Mr. George Washington (of Virginia) had served as president of the Constitutional Convention.

November 30, 1990

October 19

"**O**ctober 19," with no year attached, is Wall Street's shorthand for the market mishap of 1987. It's as if October 19, 1987, the day the Dow Jones Industrial Average dipped 508 points, a dip of 25 percent, was the only October 19 in recorded history. This essay suggests that that may be but another example of Wall Street puffery, for at least two other October 19s—1781 and 1876—must be reckoned with.

October 19, 1781 is the date that General Charles Cornwallis, commander of the British forces at the Battle of Yorktown, surrendered to General George Washington, thus ending the Revolutionary War. Wall Streeters, aware of that snippet of history, nevertheless dispute that that sword-turning-over-day can rival October 19, 1987 for genuine, permanent significance. To prove their point they note that on October 19, 1781, after the surrender had been announced on the broad tape, the Dow Jones Industrial Average moved hardly at all. There was, to be sure, some internal market response to the events in Virginia. For instance, the common shares of Schweppes and Rolls-Royce traded lower, reflecting the market's evaluation that Britain's position in the growing North American market had been weakened. Contrariwise, the shares of Perrier and Peugeot were upgraded by most brokerage houses to "buy," reflecting optimism that the earnings of French businesses in the New World would be helped by advertising campaigns that would feature endorsements by Lafayette and Rochambeau. When challenged by irate, learned historians as to how Wall Street could dare to measure everything, even the winning of our liberty, by the narrow gauge of the Dow Jones Industrial Average, an equally irate cuff-linked Big Board spokesman replied that the same conclusion would have been reached had they used the broader based Standard and Poor's 500.

Wall Street's response to October 19, 1876 was more hesitant, more difficult, for that was, as everybody knows, the birthday of baseball immortal, Hall of Fame pitcher Mordecai Peter Centennial Three-Fingers Brown. Even hard-bitten arbitrageurs acknowledge the day's transcendental importance, for his statistics (except for the placement of the decimal point) were in perfect harmony: His lifetime earned run average was 2.06 (third best in history) and his lifetime batting average was .206. Wall Street analysts love such perfect internal balance for it means, they say, that over the long term there will be no inflation. But, again, as with the Battle of Yorktown, the Dow Jones Industrials on October 19, 1876 hardly fluttered. There was, of course, the expected stock-by-stock churning. For instance, as soon as the midwife in Nyesville, Indiana announced Three-Fingers Mordecai's birth, the securities of baseball bat manufacturers declined sharply, for bats would be useless when he pitched. Frankly, I've claimed more than once that my parents were die-hard baseball fans and named me after that greatest of Chicago Cubs. It gave me some needed cachet in the schoolyard, especially since I was very short and skinny in those years. And I suppose that I may be the only one in the world who still has a glass of wine every October 19 in his honor.

The stock market crashed in 1987 because (they say) there was an unfavorable foreign trade balance and a growing national debt. In the two years since 1987 both have worsened by several hundred billion dollars. Yet the Dow Jones Industrial Average now hovers near an all-time high, as if the crash had never happened.

In the 200 years since the Battle of Yorktown we and the British have become inseparable allies, almost as if the Revolutionary War and Valley Forge had never happened.

All of which may mean that October 19s, like all the other dates on the calendar, do not much matter. Whatever happens, whether grim or joyous, is, sooner or later, undone. For as the Earth continues spinning in its old day-night-day-night routine, everything, sooner or later, will smooth out. But that may be small balm to those who lost their fortunes on October 19, 1987, for that kind of sooner or later usually means an eon or two.

October 19, 1989

X
Two Speeches
(One Irreverent)

Access
to
Justice

**Law Day Speech before the Delaware
State Bar Association (Wilmington,
Delaware, April 28, 1989)**

Mr. Chief Justice, Reverend Berry, Ladies and Gentlemen: I want to thank Bill Wiggin and Art Connolly for the great honor they have bestowed upon me by inviting me here this Law Day.

And I want to thank Bill Prickett, who most graciously encouraged my writing long before I had a publisher. It was doubly helpful because Bill is such a fine writer. And I want to thank him for that most generous but undeserved introduction. You needn't worry about my getting a swelled head because at least 25, probably closer to 35, publishers turned down my book before the University of Georgia Press accepted it for publication.

And I want to thank Joe Rosenthal and Irv Morris who so quietly contributed so much to making this day possible for me. Their participation in *Evans v. Buchanan* has said more about the access to justice than anything that I could say.

Access to Justice is a rather broad topic for a 15-minute talk, even for a class action lawyer who routinely represents tens of thousands of people he doesn't know and who never heard of him.

But if I focused the topic instead on Access to Justice in Delaware I would be presumptuous, because I know less about Delaware justice than anyone in this room.

And so I thought that my topic should be: Access to Justice in Delaware as seen by a New York lawyer. I first witnessed access to Delaware justice when I worked for a small New York firm in the mid-1950s. There I learned the strange fact that you could sue someone in Delaware even if that defendant had spent his whole life on the Planet Mars. He could be sued, provided only that he owned shares in a Delaware corporation. I refer, of course, to the old sequestration statute. That strange statute—by which the Delaware Legislature mandated that shares of a Delaware corporation existed, ghost-like, in the state of Delaware even if the certificate was safely locked in a vault a thousand miles away—that strange statute was held to be unconstitutional by the United States Supreme Court in *Shaffer v. Heitner*. The point is that access to Delaware courts and access to justice are not necessarily the same. In fact, in the *Heitner* case they were opposites.

But, of course, in the cozy ways of Delaware, the Legislature convened about 45 minutes after the *Heitner* decision was announced and enacted a new statute that accomplished the very same result, albeit constitutionally. The reason for the 45-minute delay, I'm told, is that there was a sudden, severe snow storm and the roads to Dover were blocked. But the new law was passed, and the parade of New York lawyers to Delaware continued without missing a step.

How, then, do New York lawyers, perched 75 stories high in one of those ugly glass towers—New York lawyers in firms with hundreds and hundreds of partners and with offices, all at the same time, in London, Brussels, Los Angeles, Washington, D.C., Singapore, Tokyo, Manila, Paris and Rome—how do those New Yorkers view Wilmington, Delaware? Earlier this year my wife and I saw a revival of Thornton Wilder's classic play, *Our Town*, at the Lyceum Theater in New York. *Our Town* takes place at the turn of the century in a make-believe New Hampshire town called Grovers Corners. As stated in Act I, Grovers Corners had 2,640 inhabitants. I would say that New Yorkers view Wilmington, Delaware as the Grovers Corners of the law.

Of course, Grovers Corners was not like Wilmington, Delaware in every respect. For instance, there were, in Grovers Corners, no $25 billion mergers. And there were no poison pills. Indeed, there were no lawyers in Grovers Corners, at least none appeared in the play. Which means, I suppose—although it's hard to believe—that even Skadden Arps had no office there. On the other hand, maybe Skadden Arps had no office there just because there were no offices there to raid.

But in those things that really mattered, Grovers Corners, New Hampshire and Wilmington, Delaware were and are indistinguishable. Both are not only small, but parochial. In Grovers Corners, also according to Act I, 90% of its high school graduates lived there their whole lives. Wilmington is no different. Very recently, making small talk in one of the law firms here in town, I asked a secretary when last she had visited New York. "I've never been *there*," she replied, "but I have been to Philadelphia, twice." And travel about Wilmington as one will, you will never see a picture—either an original or a copy—unless it was painted by Andrew Wyeth.

And like Grovers Corners, New Hampshire, Wilmington, Delaware has its peculiarities. Perhaps those peculiarities are seen more clearly by an outsider. For instance, no matter the facts, at least in Chancery Court, the plaintiff never wins. I don't take that personally. Every judicial system has its quirks. But it is also fair to say in that regard that Wilmington is not unique. For instance, plaintiff never wins in New York either. Or in any jurisdiction for that matter. Not, at least, since Chief Justice Earl Warren has been gone.

And, as I thought about it, the very fact of those similarities among Grovers Corners and Wilmington and New York, and every place else, is the very point of *Our Town*. Thornton Wilder was not only a playwright and a poet, but a philosopher. And the lesson—the moral lesson—of *Our Town* is that as tiny and as insular and as strange as Grovers Corners, New Hampshire may seem, people there almost a century ago had the same fears but the same hopes as people everywhere have always had. And, I suggest, if we understand that we would know what justice means and what access to justice means.

But, of course, Mr. Wilder put it more poetically. In the closing speech of *Our Town* the stage manager, who is the narrator, says as another day in Grovers Corners ends:

> There are the stars—doing
> their old, old criss-cross in
> the skies.

What the poet and playwright meant by that, I suggest, is that whether you live in Grovers Corners, New Hampshire, or Wilmington, Delaware, or New York City or Beirut, Lebanon, or Moscow or Johannesburg, we all live under those same eternal stars. And perhaps—it's just a thought for this Law Day—perhaps access to justice means letting everyone share in those stars, sharing in the starry hope that guides navigators, sharing in the starry beauty that inspires poets. So perhaps access to justice means sharing Heaven's blessings with all.

I'm going back to New York now so that when I lose my next case at least I'll be close to home.

For your great kindness in inviting me, and in listening to me, and in sharing your Law Day with me, I thank you all very much.

Time to Answer

Acceptance Speech at Touro Law School, on Receiving the First Annual Bruce K. Gould Award, April 12, 1990

Dean Glickenstein, Mr. Bruce K. Gould, Members of the Touro Law School Faculty, Students and Friends,

I am honored indeed to be the first recipient of the Bruce K. Gould Award, given for the publication of my book, *The Lament Of The Single Practitioner.* The award will not swell my head too much because I remember well that some 40 or 50 publishers turned me down before the manuscript was accepted by the University of Georgia Press.

It is a beautiful thing for a law school to give an annual award for a book; for a book, on any subject, is our civilization's most worthy object. If I speak with some feeling on the subject it is because my maternal grandfather was from a book publishing family in Vilna, and he continued that noble calling after he came to America in 1885. At the turn of the century he co-founded the Hebrew Publishing Company which published not only prayer books, but books on all Jewish themes, as well as Jewish music. And so I am honored more than I can say by this award.

The book that is the subject of the award, *The Lament Of The Single Practitioner,* received, I am happy to say, much praise, but I shall recount only one instance, the praise that it received in an essay written for the *Times* (of London) *Literary Supplement* by a Mr. Eric Korn. Although I did not respond to any other book reviews, I was so touched that my book would be mentioned in the TLS (albeit in an essay, not in a formal review) that I wrote a note to thank the author. The note was written, of course, on my office stationery, and that, as we shall see, was my undoing.

A few days later I received a response from London. Mr. Korn wrote to me and asked if, perchance, I knew of a lawyer in New York who might help him with a legal problem. Not being able to say that I knew no one, I wrote back offering to undertake the task myself, whatever it was. The only condition I imposed was that I would not, under any circumstances, accept a fee.

My offer was promptly accepted. Mr. Korn, it seemed, was not only an essayist but also an antiquarian book dealer. His book store, Dylans Book Store, located at the wonderful address of Salubrious Passage, Swansea, Wales, had participated in an Antiquarian Book Fair in New York and had sold a fine rare book to an apparently prosperous lady for $1,350. The apparently prosperous lady paid with two checks—one for $900 and one for $450—on both of which she stopped payment as soon as Mr. Korn had left New York to return home. In accepting the case, I assumed that if I wrote a lawyer letter, payment would be prompt, for why would the purchaser want to hire an attorney in so open-and-shut a case. And so I wrote a letter to the lady, who had moved to Pound Ridge, in Westchester County. My letter was ignored. And so I wrote a second, more threatening note which, like the first, was not acknowledged.

My pride was hurt, and since I had promised Mr. Korn that I would represent him, I had no choice but to begin a lawsuit. The court of appropriate jurisdiction for a case involving $1,350 plus interest was the Civil Court of New York, and I am ashamed to say that I had never before been in that Court, never once in my life. But I fancy myself to be a litigator, and so I drafted the complaint expecting the case to be an easy one. The form of the Civil Court summons is set forth in the Civil Court Act, and my secretary typed it out, word for word. The Civil Court Act provides that if a defendant resides within the 5 counties of New York City he—or in this case she—must be given 20 days to respond. But if she lives in New York State but not in New York City, the time to respond is 30 days. Since the defendant lived in Pound Ridge, in Westchester County, not in New York City, the typed summons advised her that she had to respond within 30 days or a judgment by default could be taken against her. The summons was duly served, and I waited 30 days, then 35 days, then 40 days, and finally, exasperated, I went to the Civil Court clerk's office and filed my judgment by default. That is, I left my proposed judgment in the appropriate box. But instead of a conformed copy of the judgment, I received, in about a week, a rejection. I didn't understand why, and went to the clerk for an explanation. Said he: The summons did not say that had the defendant lived in New York City she would have had only 20 days to respond. I protested that the defendant lived in Westchester County, not New York City, and that she was not only advised that she had to respond in 30 days, but that I had even given her extra time, so why did it matter that the summons did not also tell her that had she lived in New York City she would have had only 20 days to respond. "You may or may not be logically correct, Mr. Rosenfeld," intoned the clerk, "but I can't enter a default judgment when the summons never advised the defendant that had she lived in New York City she would have had to respond in 20 days."

I was in a quandary, because no matter what I did I could not change the fact that the summons said what it said. "Just serve a new summons" advised the clerk, and to play it safe I bought the printed version at the stationery store. Those blank summonses cost only 3 for $1 and I wondered why I hadn't used it the first time. The printed summons, with the same complaint attached, was duly served in Pound Ridge, and I waited 30 days, then 35 days, then 40 days, and still no response, no peep from the defendant. Again I submitted a proposed judgment by default, this time with genuine optimism. But again, in a few days, there was a rejection letter from the clerk. Again I approached the clerk, this time more timidly, and inquired why. Said he, "Mr. Rosenfeld, didn't you learn in law school that you can't amend a summons without a court order?"

Humbled again, I filed papers seeking court approval for an amended summons, *nunc pro tunc*. My motion was granted, provided that I served the papers—the summons and complaint—one more time. Again the process server was dispatched to Pound Ridge, and again I waited 30 days, 35 days, 40 days, and again, no response. Not a peep.

But this time the summons worked, and I obtained my default judgment. The problem was I didn't know what to do with it, how to enforce it, how to collect the $1,350 plus interest. By chance, those two checks that the defendant had stopped were drawn on the Irving Trust Company, my own bank. So I went to the manager of my branch and asked him if the defendant's account was still active. I was amazed to learn that there was some $3,000 still in it, so I asked the manager, a friend, how I would go about collecting on my judgment. He said that he had no idea, but referred me to the Irving Trust's lawyer, a Mr. Mancuso. I phoned Mr. Mancuso and introduced myself, and told him of my problem. When I finished, Mr. Mancuso asked, "Mr. Rosenfeld, are you really a lawyer?" I assured him that I was, and he asked when I was first admitted to the bar. I was ashamed to tell him, so I muttered something—I don't remember what—and, in order to get rid of me, he told me which forms to fill out, how many copies had to be served on the bank, and to be sure—this he repeated—to keep one copy for myself. I did exactly as told, and in a few days I received a form from the Irving Trust Company advising me that the defendant's bank account had been frozen.

And a few days later, as her checks began to bounce, I heard, for the first time, from the lady who had bought a fine, rare book from Dylan's Book Store for $1,350 but had stopped payment on the two checks she had given in exchange. She was in a panic. I told her, calmly, that all she had to do to unfreeze her bank account was to pay the full amount of the judgment, being $1,350 plus interest of $202. That afternoon, when I returned from lunch, I found an envelope with the check, for the full amount, under my door. So now I had the check, but the problem was that it was drawn on a bank account that I myself had frozen. So I called Mr. Mancuso and asked him what I could do to thaw this particular check. He couldn't believe that I didn't know what had to be done, and inquired again if I was really a lawyer. When I assured him that I was, he asked which law school I had graduated from, but I was ashamed to tell him because my particular law school, Yale, takes inordinate (but undeserved) pride in the intellectual abilities of its graduates, and so I told him that, frankly, I couldn't remember. Said Mr. Mancuso, "Mr. Rosenfeld, I'm not surprised."

Having been instructed on how to collect the money, I then did so and on the very next day I sent Mr. Korn the full amount of $1,350 plus $202 interest, being 9% a year. And as I had promised, I did not deduct any fee.

And by return mail came Mr. Korn's response from London: "Mr. Rosenfeld," his letter said, "a thousand thanks, and a thousand thanks again. You indeed must be one of the ablest lawyers in America."

Dean Glickstein and Mr. Gould, I can't tell you how much I appreciate the great honor you have bestowed upon me. And thank you all—a thousand thanks, as Mr. Korn would say—for sharing this wonderful occasion with me.